Harvard Studies in Romance Languages: 34

A Genetic Approach to Structures
in the Work of Jean Genet

A Genetic Approach to Structures in the Work of Jean Genet

Camille Naish

Distributed for the
Department of Romance Languages and Literatures
of Harvard University by
Harvard University Press
Cambridge, Massachusetts
1978

Library of Congress Cataloging in Publication Data

Naish, Camille, 1945-

A genetic approach to structures in the work
of Jean Genet.

(Harvard studies in Romance languages; 34)
Bibliography: p.
1. Genet, Jean, 1910-   -- Criticism and
interpretation. I. Title.   II. Series.
PQ2613.E53Z79   848'.9'1209   78-7059
ISBN 0-674-34581-9

ACKNOWLEDGEMENTS

The present study is based on a doctoral dissertation written in 1972-4 under the direction of Germaine Brée, then Vilas Professor of French at the Institute for Research in the Humanities, University of Wisconsin. For her patience and encouragement I am exceedingly grateful.

I should like to thank Mme Leonor Fini, MM Roger Blin and Constantin Jelenski for interviews graciously accorded, and Mme Célia Bertin-Reich and the late Olivier Picard for strategic assistance.

At Harvard University I wish particularly to thank Dorrit Cohn, Professor of German, for her invaluable suggestions as to the revision of the original manuscript; Donald A. Stone, Jr., Professor of Romance Languages and Literatures, for his practical help and meticulous corrections; and Laurence W. Wylie, C. Douglas Dillon Professor of the Civilization of France, for most kindly sponsoring this publication under the rules pertaining to the Solomon Lincoln Fund.

Camille Naish
Cambridge, Massachusetts
June 7, 1978

For Germaine Brée

CONTENTS

x

INTRODUCTION: GENET, POET-THIEF

> "...ce n'est pas ce
> que j'ai vécu, mais le ton
> sur lequel je le rapporte..."
>
> Jean Genet,
> Journal du voleur.

> C'est seulement ces
> sortes de vérités, celles
> qui ne sont pas démontrables
> et même qui sont "fausses,"
> celles que l'on ne peut
> conduire sans absurdité
> jusqu'à leur extrémité sans
> aller à la négation d'elles
> et de soi, c'est celles-là
> qui doivent être exaltées
> par l'oeuvre d'art. Elles
> n'auront jamais la chance
> ni la malchance d'être un
> jour appliquées. Qu'elles
> vivent par le chant qu'elles
> sont devenues et qu'elles
> suscitent.
>
> Jean Genet,
> Ce qui est resté d'un Rem-
> brandt déchiré en petits
> carrés bien réguliers, et
> foutu aux chiottes.

In September 1942, printed on wretched paper and with copious typographical errors, a poem appeared in Fresnes. It was lugubriously entitled Le Condamné à mort, and its publication initiated the literary career of Jean Genet, a poet, imprisoned at that time in Fresnes. One year later, Jean Cocteau was to declare Genet France's greatest living writer. This startling judgement was addressed in July 1943 to the Dix-neuvième Chambre Correctionnelle in Paris, where Genet was being tried for stealing books, including expensive editions of Cocteau himself and Verlaine. Cocteau's laudatory verdict deferred the life sentence of preventive detention which Genet risked incurring; it also constituted the first and doubtless the most memorable appraisal of the younger poet's work. During the next thirty years Jean Genet's abject obscurity yielded to literary notoriety as critical squalls and public scandals broke out with many of his subsequent publications. Throughout this unusual career Genet appears to have consistently considered himself a poet; poetry was the first literary form he chose, and poet he chooses to term himself even in his novels and his essays, even when prefacing his plays.

In April 1944 the long fragment of a novel, Notre-Dame-des-Fleurs, appeared in Marc Barbezat's periodical L'Arbalète. In September of that year publication of the novel in its entirety was paid for by anonymous "amateurs" in Monte Carlo. Other works succeeded: volumes of poetry in 1945 and 1948; a second novel, Miracle de la Rose, in 1946. 'Adame Miroir, a short "ballet-scenario," was performed in Paris in 1946, and also a play, Les Bonnes; a second play - actually written first - Haute Surveillance was produced in 1949. The two plays were profitable to Genet both as poet and as thief, bringing him the Prix de la Pléiade and several rich acquaintances. In 1947, a year in which other wealthy "amateurs" published two additional novels, Pompes funèbres and Querelle de Brest,

Genet was summoned to the courts again, this
time receiving sentence of detention for life.
Sartre, who had met Genet as early as 1944
through Cocteau and Mme Barbezat, thereupon
mobilised Parisian intelligentsia on his behalf;
a group of writers, including Cocteau, Mauriac
and Mondor, appealed to then President Vincent
Auriol. Not only was Genet pardoned and set
free, but he was invited to dinner at the
Elysées.

At about this time, fragments of his
Journal du voleur were appearing in Les Temps
Modernes; dedicated to Sartre and Simone de
Beauvoir, this apparent autobiography was published first anonymously, then commercially by
Gallimard in 1949. Journal du voleur is both a
rather intellectualised account of a literary
enterprise and a farewell to literature, for its
author seems resolved not to write any more. In
1952, as if to consecrate this valedictory tone,
Gallimard published the monumental Saint-Genet,
comédien et martyr, an introduction, of some six-
hundred pages, which Sartre wrote for the forthcoming Oeuvres Complètes of Jean Genet. Between
1948 and 1956 there was, indeed, a cessation of
activity; Genet wrote, only a few essays, elegant
but brief, on Cocteau, on the paintress Leonor
Fini, on delinquent children. Having seen his
soul laid bare in the prehensile manuscript of
Sartre, Genet, as he later confessed, almost
gave up writing. Cocteau for his part feared,
of Saint-Genet, that Genet emerged from it "plus
canonné que canonisé," more martyrised than
sanctified. "C'est un des plus émouvants mystè-
res que celui-ci," observed Genet himself in
1958; "après une période brillante, tout artiste
aura traversé une désepérante contrée, risquant
de perdre sa raison et sa maitrise; S'il sort
vainqueur..."[1] Fortunately Genet did emerge
victorious. Between 1956 and 1961 he composed
three great plays - Le Balcon, Les Nègres and
Les Paravents - his best-known essays (L'Atelier
d'Alberto Giacometti, Le Funambule) and several
pieces on theatrical aesthetics. In 1966 his

last play, <u>Les Paravents</u>, caused riots at the
Théâtre National de l'Odéon; police protection
was accorded Roger Blin, the director, and
actors of the Renaud-Barrault troupe; Genet was
awarded the Prix du Palmarès for the year's best
play. In 1968 Genet popped up in Chicago, having
entered the United States illegally for the purpose of attending the Democratic National Convention; <u>Esquire</u> commissioned the satirical
impressions published in November of that year.
In 1971, under the auspices of <u>Tel Quel</u>, Genet
gave a series of lectures on the Black Panthers
to Parisian audiences. It seems safe to say
that since the publication, in 1968, of several
literary essays in the fourth volume of his
<u>Oeuvres Complètes</u>, Genet has definitively re-
nounced literature for politics.

Dates, titles, and the names of Barbezat
and Gallimard - such is the information which
first and most readily presents itself in a critical study of Genet. Given the exact nature of
his literary adventure, such studies are liable
rapidly to turn into analyses of Legend. It is
in <u>Journal du voleur</u> that Genet most stresses
the legendary aspect of his undertaking:

> Depuis cinq ans j'écris des livres;
> je peux dire que je l'ai fait avec
> plaisir mais j'ai fini. Par l'écri-
> ture j'ai obtenu ce que je cherchais.
> Ce qui, m'étant un enseignement,
> me guidera, ce n'est pas ce que j'ai
> vécu mais le ton sur lequel je le
> rapporte. Non les anecdotes, mais
> l'oeuvre d'art. Non ma vie, mais
> son interprétation. C'est ce qui
> m'offre le langage pour parler
> d'elle, la traduire. Réussir ma
> légende.[2]

Elsewhere in the same book, underlining the ety-
mological link between "legendary" and legible,"
he writes: "légende, c'est-à-dire lisible," and
indeed, a number of passages in the <u>Journal</u>

summarise in similar terms his five-year intellectual effort. The success of his legend was
accompanied by a degree of vulgarisation. In
1951 a Gallimard publicist declared that Genet's
name had unquestionably become a legend; "Jamais,"
proclaims the blurb for <u>Oeuvres Complètes, II</u>,
"écrivain n'a eu si grande notoriété en si peu
de temps." It was his notoriety which first
attracted the attention of his contemporaries,
certain of whom, in their retrospectively composed <u>mémoires</u>, express reservations as to the
label "poet-thief" affixed to Genet promptly
upon his "discovery." Violette Leduc, for example, recalls how in 1944 she read in a newspaper
that the poet-thief was out of prison, that
Cocteau was helping him:

> Qui était-ce, ce Jean Genet dont je
> n'avais rien lu, dont on n'avait
> rien publié? Le mot voleur, accouplé
> à celui de poète, me déplaisait.
> Genet, ainsi étiqueté, me paraissait
> avec la lavallière d'Aristide Bruant.[3]

It seems that the first person to speak of Genet
to Sartre and Simone de Beauvoir was Olga
Barbezat, the printer's wife, herself interned
a while in Fresnes with members of the French
Resistance;

> Il avait été recueilli à sa naissance
> par l'Assistance publique et placé
> chez des paysans; la majeure partie
> de son enfance s'était passée dans
> des maisons de correction; il avait
> beaucoup volé et cambriolé à travers
> le monde et il était pédéraste. En
> prison, il avait lu; il avait composé
> des vers puis un livre; Olga Barbezat
> disait de lui monts et merveilles. Je
> m'en laissais moins conter que dans ma
> jeunesse; le voyou de génie me semblait
> un personnage un peu conventionnel...[4]

After reading the first published fragments of

<u>Notre-Dame-des-Fleurs</u>, however, Mme de Beauvoir
was convinced of Genet's talent. Pronouncing his
style unique and inimitable, despite visible
influences of Proust, Cocteau and Jouhandeau,
she even declares that these fragments renewed
her faith in literature, restoring words to all
their pristine power.

Nevertheless, not all critical reactions
to Genet's work were so enthusiastic. Sartre
observes that the Surrealists - he does not specify which ones - were greatly irritated by
Genet's "eulogy" of treason. The slim volumes of
poetry - <u>Chants secrets</u> of 1945 and <u>Poèmes</u> of 1948 -
did not inspire a single favourable review. When
<u>Les Bonnes</u> was performed at the Théâtre de
l'Athénée in April 1947[5] it was bitterly attacked
by Robert Kemp, the critic from <u>Le Monde</u>; Thierry
Maulnier, on the other hand, praised it to the
skies. When, in 1949, <u>Haute Surveillance</u> was put
on at the Théâtre des Mathurins, a violent conflict broke out between Jean Marchat, director of
the theatre, and Jean-Jacques Gauthier, drama critic of the <u>Figaro</u> and a future Academician. Shortly thereafter François Mauriac wrote a violent
and subsequently famous denunciation in <u>Le Figaro
Littéraire</u>; entitled "Le Cas Jean Genet," his
article accused the "Orpheus of Vice" of using
his considerable talent to exploit depravity.
Situating Genet rather vaguely in Rimbaldian
tradition, Mauriac commends Rimbaud for the good
Catholic modesty which prompted the latter's
timely silence and, Mauriac opines, abandonment
of literature.

An important part of Genet's work became
publicly available in 1951 and 1953 when Gallimard published two volumes of his Complete Works,
containing the four novels and three poems. This
did little to modify the critical polarities already apparent in 1947. A few humanists, such
as J.-J. Riniéri and Roger Stéphane, defended the
singular universe Genet had created, a universe
in which man pursued a solitary and a tragic destiny. The Catholic establishment, as represented

by André Rousseaux, Pierre de Boisdeffre and
Gabriel Marcel, recognised the elegance and
sumptuosity of Genet's style but abhorred his
sordid themes - homosexuality, theft, betrayal
- and his manner of exalting sanctity as attained through the inverse asceticism of crime.
They also deplored his "scandalous exploitation,"
in Les Nègres and Les Paravents, of fashionable
political themes. For more than a decade, however, French criticism of Genet was dominated by
the ponderous tome of Saint-Genet, comédien et
martyre.

Curiously enough, it is debatable to
what extent Sartre's huge opus actually constitutes literary criticism, so far does it exceed
the normal confines of aesthetic or ideological
commentary. Saint-Genet is simultaneously a
kind of novel, a demonstration of existential
psychoanalysis, a marxian critique of feudal
consumer societies, a literary exegesis, dialectical explication of sodomy, essay in thematic
criticism, essay in historical speculation and
scolium on the lives of saints. As in his study
of Baudelaire, as in Les Mots, Sartre attempts
to reconstruct and reinterpret the events and
psychological climate which caused a small boy
to become a writer - indeed, not merely a writer
but the writer of that particular talent and
renown recognised by the names of Genet, Sartre
and Baudelaire. Although Sartre freely avails
himself of Genet's texts to aid his re-creation,
the process he employs is a novelistic one,
comparable even to that of Proust in A la recherche du temps perdu. Sartre attempts to explain
in biographical terms what is normally understood, rather vaguely it is true, by the word
"genius." Essential to the Sartrian thesis are
the concepts of choice andliberty, both of which
Genet apparently exercised in resolutely willing
himself to become the thief and pederast others
thought him to be. When Genet's active choice
evolved into a will to do evil, Sartre maintains,
he became a sort of parasite, living off "good"
just as the word "evil" necessarily implies its

opposite. Later on, the better to corrupt his
Honest Bourgeois Readers with his gorgeous wicked
prose, Genet became a writer. From a purely
literary standpoint, one of the more interesting
parts of Saint-Genet is the analysis of Genet's
poems, which Sartre deems prosaic; according to
him Genet's real poetry lives parasitically in
his novels, eroding rational, significant prose
just as Evil corrupts Good. Towards the end of
his "monument," Sartre transforms Genet into the
stereotype martyr of subjectivity, an equivalent
to Bokharin in the U.S.S.R. who by similar tokens
becomes the martyr of objective consciousness.
Sartre's canonisation is accordingly ambivalent,
since the martyrdoms of both Genet and Bokharin
seem equally vain and fruitless; moreover, as
Sartre readily admits, six hundred pages written
on a living author in effect entomb him.

In 1957 Georges Bataille devoted a long-
ish chapter to Genet in La Littérature et le mal.
His study, which treats actively of Saint-Genet
and rather less of Genet, does not add much to
existing criticism of the poet. As Bataille has
a tendency to refer everything to his own socio-
anthropological theories of communication, his
conclusion is not especially optimistic: "Genet,
qui écrit, n'ai ni le pouvoir ni l'intention de
communiquer avec ses lecteurs."[6] In 1956 appeared
Claude Bonnefoy's Genet, a thematic exposé of the
novels, the Journal and the plays, with auxiliary
reference to the poems and the major essays. In
1966 Jean-Marie Magnan published a nice essay,
Pour un blason de Jean Genet, in the Collection
Seghers. As its title indicates, this study extracts themes and images from Genet's texts -
including Le Condamné à mort, Le Funambule and
L'Atelier d'Alberto Giacometti - to create an
emblematic portrait of the poet. Although not
wholly of a Sartrian descent, these two works
remain introductory in nature, and do not contribute to a detailed understanding of Genet's technical procedures. More recently, Lucien Goldmann
has written a series of sociological articles re-
lating Genet's theatre to the collective politi-

cal unconscious of western European society. Of
Genet's last three dramas, M. Goldmann postulates:

> ...il nous semble pour le moins possi-
> ble que la structure fondamentale de
> ces trois pièces corresponde à la
> structure mentale et psychique qui
> n'est pas consciente et en tout cas
> pas toujours exprimée, d'une partie
> importante de la gauche radicale
> française...[7]

More particularly, M. Goldmann has applied his
method to Les Paravents, tracing Saïd's obsti-
nate fall through the three social orders of the
play, and suggesting that Genet's last major
work may herald a new moment in Western dramatic
consciousness.

        If Genet's French critics have tended to
stress the moral, metaphysical and socio-politi-
cal content of his work, anglo-american scholar-
ship, unabashed, has made strides in the realm of
aesthetic commentary. An important early contri-
bution came in 1963, a year in which the Grove
Press published commercial translations of Saint-
Genet and Notre-Dame-des-Fleurs; Joseph McMahon
chose this moment to present Genet's novels and
plays to an English-speaking public. His book,
The Imagination of Jean Genet, emphasises the
originality of Genet's creative invention and
also establishes a distinction between two operative imaginative faculties: the instinctive and
the representative. According to McMahon, the
reader's critical intelligence enables him to
reject the conclusions of the first while his
aesthetic sensibility is ravished by the second.
This distinction does tend to be rejected by the
Sartrian critics, who resolutely maintain that
to read Genet is to ally oneself with Evil. Nonetheless, Professor McMahon's book does not contain
the extended analysis of the imaginative process
implied by its title.

        In 1968 two British professors, Richard

Coe and Philip Thody, published the first truly
"academic" works on Genet. That is to say -
lest the term "academic" seem a trifle biased -
that both critics consider such matters as the
chronology of Genet's work, the evolution of its
themes, images and language, viewed as consti-
tuent parts of literary expression, rather than
as sociological documents or eccentricities to
be perused by a psychologist. Accompanied by
excellent bibliographical notes, these two
studies evidence comprehensive research. They
differ in that Mr Thody accepts neither the
Sartrian dialectic which permeates Mr Coe's
fluid prose, nor the Sartrian concept of the
Honest Man; this imaginary reader, Thody thinks,
is a fictitious and hopelessly reactionary
creation. Thody lays interesting emphasis on
Genet's own critical faculty which, related to
his humour and his solid common sense, counter-
balances his rhetoric and his Romantic tendencies.
Richard Coe, endeavoring to situate Genet with
respect to contemporary western culture, recognises all manner of contradictions in his work:

> Revolutionary or reactionary? Both.
> Realist or mystic? Both. Symbolist
> or existentialist? Both. Tradition-
> alist or avant-garde? Here, even
> more disquietingly, the answer seems
> to be the inevitable: both.[8]

This proto-conclusion is typical of Mr Coe, who
constantly perceives in Genet's writing a dynamic
opposition of two Sartrian fundamentals, Being
and Nothingness. This dialectic opposition -
manifest, in psychological terms, in the reflection of opposing consciousnesses - is resolved,
according to Mr Coe, in the re-reflection of a
third consciousness. The resulting "Trinities"
are ably assimilated, in Mr Coe's disquisition,
to the theological overtones of Genet's work.
It is questionable, however, that Genet, although
acquainted with Sartre since May 1944, created
his characteristic Trinities in the full pleni-
tude of existential deliberation which Richard
Coe seems to imply.

Anglo-American critics have also contrib-
uted numerous articles and several books on
Genet's theatre, which they tend to categorise,
together with works by Beckett and Ionesco, as
Theatre of the Absurd. American universities
have also produced a dozen or so dissertations
treating of diverse aspects of Genet's dramas -
the element of ritual, "surrealist" distancing,
the theme of death, the function of irony. A
single thesis has concerned itself primarily with
Genet's novels: that of Barbara Gerber, who has
analysed the fictional metamorphosis - at once
alchemical, mythical and ironic - whereby Genet's
life becomes artistic legend. Her study, which
is somewhat Jungian in parts, treats further of
the role of objects in the novels and Les Paravents.

Contemporary or "New" French criticism
has in the early seventies devoted a few signal
publications to Genet. In October 1972 a special
issue of the drama periodical Obliques dealt with
Genet's plays; included with the standard best
in French and American articles were two essays,
by Jean Gitenet and Michèle Piemme, on stage
directions in Le Balcon, tableau 4, and on space
and illusion in that play. In 1974 Jacques
Derrida published Glas, a slightly confusing tome
whose typographical configurations curiously
resemble those of Genet's own Rembrandt essay,
published in 1967; two columns of text, printed
side by side upon the page, treat of apparently
unrelated phenomena. At moments, however, it
does seem that Derrida discusses names, tombs,
executions and signatures as they occur in Genet's
diverse writings.

Considering the large critical corpus I
have briefly reviewed, one might reasonably infer
that everything has now been said regarding Jean
Genet, poet-thief and contemporary laureate.
This is not at all the case. Despite a body of
articles, and several chapters in books, conse-
created to the shape and the form - "play within
a play" - and illusionism of Genet's dramas, very

little criticism has traced structural similarities between the plays; still less has related
these structures to the essential forms of his
novels. The general critical tendency is to view
Genet's novels as a sort of onanistic indulgence,
the depressing, self-enclosed reflection of a
literary solitude; his dramas, on the other hand,
destined for public representation and often political in theme, are seen as steps towards re-
generation.[9] In fact, structural resemblances
obtain between almost all Genet's works - poems,
plays and novels.

A characteristic of Genet's early poems
is their duality. This quality reflects the
facts of circumstance and content; incarcerated
in a cell at Fresnes, the poet in turn holds his
protagonists prisoner within his poems. As the
poet becomes aware of this parallelism - which
is really a paradoxical inversion of his own loss
of liberty - he incorporates it, self-consciously,
into the themes of the poem. In other words, the
creation of the poem emerges as the subject of
the poem. This is particularly apparent in
Genet's second opuscule, Marche funèbre. The
same paradoxical duality marks Genet's first two
novels, Notre-Dame-des-Fleurs and Miracle de la
Rose; again, these works claim to have been composed in prison. To mention the biography of
poets is to violate a canon of contemporary
criticism which rules that the literary work is
detached from its author - to the extent, one
might sometimes feel tempted to observe, of
writing itself without him. Accordingly, I
attempt to mention only such circumstantial
facts as seem to assist the explanation of a
given text's genesis.

A genetic approach[10] attempts to analyse
the processes by which a work comes into existence or is "engendered." Such an endeavour
appears far from modest, and was indeed rejected
by the Russian Formalist Tynianov, on the grounds
that the notion of "genesis" belongs to a system
of references outside the text. However, as

Tzvetan Todorov has subsequently argued, certain
aspects of the discipline of literary history
are essential to a comprehension of certain
texts:

> Mais une telle affirmation (that is,
> the irrelevance of genesis) se heurte
> à deux objections qui, curieusement,
> furent également formulées en premier
> par le même Tynianov. Dans une étude
> sur la "Théorie de la parodie," il
> avait montré l'impossibilité de com-
> prendre intégralement un texte de
> Dostoïevski sans se référer à tel
> texte antérieur de Gogol. C'est à
> la suite de ce travail que commencèrent
> les recherches sur ce qu'on a appelé
> ici le registre polyvalent (ou dia-
> logique). Il en découle que la genèse
> est inséparable de la structure,
> l'histoire de la création du livre,
> de son sens: si on ignorait la
> fonction parodique du texte dostoïev-
> skien (à première vue, simple élément
> de genèse), sa compréhension en souf-
> frirait gravement.[11]

It happens that a further element of Genet's
writing which has been somewhat ignored is,
precisely, the parodical aspects of several plays
and Notre-Dame-des-Fleurs. As a literary genre,
parody implies duality in as much as it involves
the more or less burlesque imitation of a well-
known work of art (in the case of Notre-Dame,
the Holy Bible). It thus supposes two inter-
dependent orders: the implicit order of the
original, parodied model; and the explicit order
of the actual parody. This duality is not unlike that of satire, a slightly more astringent
genre which, in ridiculing the foibles and vices
of mankind, tends to point rather drastically
towards the gap between the "ideal" and the "real"
as perceived by the satirical author.

Indirectly related to parody is the matter
of Genet's eclecticism, of literary borrowings.

The question of influences too, appealed in its
way to the Formalists:

> C'est grâce aux Formalistes russes
> que l'on a commencé à reconnaître
> l'importance de ce trait du langage.
> Chklovski écrivait déjà: 'L'oeuvre
> d'art est perçue en relation avec
> les autres oeuvres artistiques et à
> l'aide d'associations qu'on fait avec
> elles... Non seulement le pastiche
> mais toute oeuvre d'art est créée en
> parallèle et en opposition à un modèle
> quelconque.[12]

It is clear from the abundance of cultural references in Notre-Dame-des-Fleurs alone that Genet
acquired, in the course of his delinquent vaga-
bondage across Europe, a fairly extensive knowledge of literature and art. This cultural
versatility is generally explained by the fact
that he read prodigiously in prison. Bearing in
mind the immense difficulty of ascertaining
exactly what he read when, I have chosen briefly
to discuss relevant affinities for certain texts.

All through his unconventional literary
career, Genet refers to himself as a poet, which
seems logical if one considers that his first
writings took the form of verse. For Sartre,
these verses nonetheless constitute an additional
paradox: they are prosaic. Genet's real poetry,
Sartre maintains, erupts in his prose, whose
grammatical norms are secretly perverted by
erotic or criminal implication. Rephrasing this,
one might say that the horizontal syntagmatic
or prosaic axis is violated by vertical homo-
erotic metaphor: Notre-Dame-des-Fleurs, Miracle
de la Rose, Pompes funèbres are ambiguous titles
which contain metaphors predominant in those
three novels, to give an evident example. There
are, however, other ways in which the notion of
poetry is expressed in Genet's works; the most
important is the idiom of song. Repeatedly, song
is invoked as a lyrical artifice, a pretext for

literary effusion, corresponding to highly emotional states of mind. Hence Le Condamné à mort
becomes the song of the condemned man, while the
"Divine-Sage" of Notre-Dame-des-Fleurs is conceived as a kind of chant: "Puisque Divine est
morte, le poète peut la chanter..."[13] Even in
Querelle de Brest, the most "objective" of
Genet's novels - it has no narrating, incarcerated
Jean Genet - song enters the narrative by means of
a popular refrain, a sort of theme-song for the
hero Georges Querelle. In several of Genet's
plays, song is present not merely in snatches
of refrain or in lyrical emission but also as a
theme, an element of plot; in Le Balcon, for
example, the renegade prostitute Chantal sings
for the revolutionaries as they storm the govern-
mental barricades. The effect of this melodic
preoccupation is to create an inner equivalent to
the text itself, and so to reinforce the structural
peculiarity whereby the work of art stands revealed
as its own subject.

NOTES TO INTRODUCTION

[1] Jean Genet, Le Funambule in Les Bonnes &
L'Atelier d'Alberto Giacometti (Lyon:
L'Arbalète, 1958), p. 203.

[2] Jean Genet, Journal du voleur (Paris: Gallimard, 1949), pp. 217-8.

[3] Violette Leduc, La Folie en tête (Paris: Gallimard, 1970), p. 31.

[4] Simone de Beauvoir, La Force de l'Age (Paris:
Gallimard, 1960), p. 494.

[5] Dates given for the first performance of Les
Bonnes vary slightly. The generally accepted
date is April 19, 1947; but Richard N. Coe
(The Vision of Jean Genet, New York: The Grove
Press, 1968) gives April 17, 1946.

[6] Georges Bataille, La littérature et le mal
(Paris: Gallimard, 1957), p. 219.

[7] Lucien Goldmann, "Le Théâtre de Genet," in
Structures mentales et création culturelle
(Paris: Editions Anthropos, 1970), p. 328.

[8] Richard N. Coe, The Vision of Jean Genet,
p. 313.

[9] See for example Jacques Ehrmann, "Genet's
Dramatic Metamorphosis: From Appearance to
Freedom," Yale French Studies 29, Spring-
Summer 1962, pp. 33-42.

[10] The pun is regrettable. Genet himself was well
aware of the multiple possibilities of his name,
and seems to alternate between "broom" and
"horse."

18

[11]T. Todorov, _Poétique_ (Paris: Seuil, 1968),
p. 92-3. English parenthesis mine.

[12]Todorov, _Poétique_, p. 44.

[13]Jean Genet, _Notre-Dame-des-Fleurs_ in _Oeuvres Complètes II_ (Paris: Gallimard, 1951), p. 24.

CHAPTER I: THREE POEMS OF JEAN GENET

(a) Introduction

The poems of Jean Genet have been but infrequently examined by critics who tend to dismiss them as obscene, depressing and inferior. In 1951 the Catholic critic André Rousseaux, reviewing the first volume of the Gallimard Oeuvres Complètes, castigated Genet for his immoral themes and declared the poetry to be that of a corrupt and mediocre Lamartine. More recently, the Australian critic Richard Coe has termed these first writings "gratuitous lyric effusions which spring to the surface of Genet's mind without justification and consequently without effect." [1] Genet himself reportedly dislikes his own poems, finding them "too much influenced by Cocteau and neo-classicism"[2] - an ironic disclaimer, considering that Cocteau once declared Genet "France's greatest living writer" largely on the basis of these texts. Whatever one may think of these pronouncements, they remain almost unique. Only Sartre, in a chapter of Saint-Genet, attempts a prolonged analysis of two better-known poems. The result is both humorous and enlightening, but belongs to the overall existential hypothesis which informs that lengthy book. Even Sartre does not explore the structural links between the first poems and Genet's subsequent works.

Jean Genet wrote six published poems of which the first, Le Condamné à mort, appeared in a rather humble edition at Fresnes in 1942. This publication may be said to mark the beginning of Genet's literary career. It was followed by numerous editions, some pirated, some anonymous, some luxurious, of various combinations of the six poems. Of these, the most significant printings were those of Marc Barbezat - Chants secrets in 1945 and Poèmes in 1948 - and the collector's edition of La Galère, published by J. Loyau in 1947 with erotic illustrations by Leonor Fini. The Barbezat edition of 1948 comprises all six works, actually written before 1945, and is probably the most reliable.

Since the greater part of Genet's verse
was composed in prison, it does not seem extraordinary that four of the six items relate explicitly to aspects of the penal life. Like
the novel Notre-Dame-des-Fleurs, the first two
poems, Le Condamné à mort and Marche funèbre,
were written in or before 1942; the novel and
Le Condamné bear dedications to Maurice Pilorge,
a murderer and blond Apollo beheaded in his
twentieth year while pulling faces at the executioner. The presence of Pilorge pervades all
three works, which culminate in the apotheoses
by decapitation of criminal adolescents. In
Genet's third published poem, La Galère, the
slave galley of the title becomes an oneiric
symbol of erotic release, concomitant with its
factual function of transporting convicts to
French Guiana; for Genet, this warm and distant
land has furthermore the attributes of pederastic
Paradise. Although probably written some time
before Genet's second novel, Miracle de la Rose,[3]
La Galère has certain links with the prose work;
both are dominated by the mystical presence of
the killer Harcamone, both make metaphoric use
of the "rose." Miracle de la Rose, moreover,
contains passages in which the narrator dreams
of perpetrating erotic misdeeds aboard a slave
ship. Le Condamné à mort and La Galère are
probably the best known of Genet's poems, having
been re-edited the most frequently, and having
evident thematic ties with the novels mentioned.
But it is important also to mention the remaining texts of the 1948 edition: La Parade, which
treats of an imaginary massacre of adolescents
in a fictional penitentiary; Un Chant d'Amour;
and Le Pêcheur du Suquet. The last two were
written at a time when Genet was much in love
with Lucien Sénémaud, a young anomaly in the
poet's life who had only the most tenuous connections with the world of petty crime.

The six poems enumerated do not in fact
constitute Genet's initial venture into verse.
At the age of sixteen the delinquent waif Jean
Genet was taken up and sheltered by a blind bard,

René de Buxeuil, for whom he apparently acted as
a human guide dog. It is thought that Buxeuil,
a composer of royalist ballads of a particularly
moral and sentimental species, taught his protégé
the rudiments of prosody and metrics. Four years
later, according to Sartre, Genet wrote a poem
which he subsequently lost or destroyed: "J'avais
vingt ans; dix ans plut tôt une fillette que
j'aimais était morte et c'était l'anniversaire
de sa mort. J'écrivis ces vers pour m'émouvoir."[4]
As far as we know, this effort was not repeated
for another ten years, when, aged approximately
thirty, Genet was to write Le Condamné à mort.
There exists a gruesome and problematical octosyllable to which Genet alludes in Journal du
voleur: "Le premier vers que je m'étonnai
d'avoir formé c'est celui-ci: 'Moissonneur des
souffles coupés.' Ce que j'écrivis plus haut me
le rappelle." [5] This curious line, which Sartre
has termed a verbal pudding-stone, is recalled to
the narrator of Journal by his own descriptions
of two landscapes; the first, a field of rye,
ripe and of an heraldic gold, across which ran
the Polish border; the second, a nocturnal French
countryside, haunted by sinister reminiscences of
Vacher, the criminal who slaughtered shepherd
boys. Whether or not one chooses to accept as
real Genet's accounts of these poetic geneses,
they do reflect in literary wise a certain desire
in the poet to be moved by what he wrote, besides
a preoccupation with morbid themes. The episode
of the octosyllable further reveals the poet's
own awareness of his imaginative power: the
ability to perceive corresponding elements in
two apparently disparete scenes, to cause them
to fuse in a single yet composite image - the
ability, in short, to draw metaphor from analogy.

As for René de Buxeuil, it is both tempting and possible to accredit him with influences
in form and tone, reflected in Genet's odd but
rigorous manipulation of the alexandrine, and in
a certain amorous sentimentality which, often
dependant on the private magic of anatomical evocations, appears almost an obscene travesty of

his protector's effusive calendar lyrics.

(b) Le Condamné à mort and Marche funèbre

Of the poetic genesis of Le Condamné à
mort, Jean Genet has provided two retrospective
accounts; they appear at first reading slightly
contradictory and may even both be purely fictional. The first of the two versions, chronologically speaking, constitutes a minuscule part
of the plot of Genet's second novel, Miracle de
la Rose, where it is presented as a part of the
epistolary intercourse between the narrator
Genet and the semi-literate burglar Bulkaen:

> De Bulkaen je reçus encore un mot
> en échange du mien... Il me deman-
> dait d'écrire quelques vers sur un
> sujet qu'il me donnait; "Jean, veux-
> tu me faire des vers là-dessus:
> deux amis qui se sont beaucoup aimés
> en prison, il y en a un qui s'en va.
> Celui qui reste lui écrit pour lui
> dire qu'il l'aimera toujours et
> qu'il attend d'aller le rejoindre
> même au bagne où ils seront heureux"...
>
> Ces lignes entre mes doigts! ... si
> l'on me vola ma mort, sa mort vola
> son destin, c'est Bulkaen que j'avais
> prévu au milieu des fougères, quand
> j'écrivis le Condamné à mort.[6]

The second version, which corroborates the biographical interpretation prevalent throughout
Saint-Genet, was ostensibly narrated to Sartre
by Genet himself:

> On me poussa dans une cellule où
> se trouvaient déjà plusieurs détenus
> en vêtements 'de ville'...Or, il y
> avait parmi eux un détenu qui faisait
> des poèmes à sa soeur; poèmes idiots
> et pleurnichards qu'ils admiraient
> beaucoup. A la fin, agacé, je déclarai

> que je serais capable d'en faire
> autant. Ils me mirent au défi et
> j'écrivis le <u>Condamné à mort</u>; je
> le leur lus un jour et ils ne firent
> que me mépriser davantage; je
> terminai la lecture au milieu des
> insultes et des railleries...[7]

This latter anecdote, which reads like a parody
of some poetic concourse, might appear to be the
more authentic, since it is not recounted in an
obvious fictional narrative. It is, however,
possible that Sartre, in choosing thus to illustrate Genet's supposed aspirations after negation incarnate, unconsciously suggested to the
poet a re-interpretation of the legendary transition from convict into scribe. In fact the two
versions complete each other, the second merely
adding circumstance to theme; both evince a
tendency to render slightly mythical, through an
additional textual reference, the original
moment of composition.

The dedication of <u>Le Condamné</u> actually
contains all that is essential for the comprehension of that opuscule. It may even be considered
as a third, pertinent account of how the poem
came to be written:

> J'ai dédié ce poème à la mémoire de
> mon ami Maurice Pilorge dont le corps
> et le visage hantent mes nuits sans
> sommeil. En esprit je revis avec lui
> les quarante jours qu'il passa, les
> chaines aux pieds et parfois aux
> poignets, dans la cellule des condamnés
> à mort à la prison de Saint-Brieuc.[8]

The poet's own explanation of <u>Le Condamné</u> is
thus presented in terms of a vigil, a poetic surveillance of the man condemned to death.

Placed after the poem itself, the dedication also contains the erroneous information that
Pilorge was decapitated on March 17, 1939, a
blunder of some precision which has been quoted

as a critical caution against Genet's deceptive
exactitude. Fortunately it matters little that
the date is wrong, since the dedication may be
seen as a sort of textual appendage, a self-
conscious frame which justifies and implicitly
contains the metric fact of the poem. It is a
retrospective statement of intent; reacting dis-
dainfully to journalistic banalities of the order
of "Que cet enfant eût été digne d'un autre
destin," Genet clearly conceives of the poem as
an affirmation:

> Bref on le ravala. Pour moi,
> qui l'ai connu et qui l'ai aimé,
> je veux ici, le plus doucement
> possible, tendrement, affirmer
> qu'il fut digne, par la double
> et unique splendeur de son âme
> et de son corps, d'avoir le bénéfice
> d'une telle mort.
>
> (Poèmes, p. 27)

Despite its various evident elegiac qualities,
it would seem that Le Condamné was intended as
a Luciferian demonstration rather than a Lycidian
lament.

The poem, in its metrical aspect, con-
sists of sixty-two quatrains of regular alexandrines, plus four stanzas equiped with supernumary
hemistiches. It is divided into five lyrical
movements, corresponding to thematic phases, the
arrangement of which is respected in the Barbezat
editions. The movements are cyclic in structure
and sexual in content. I indicate the latter
particular since these structural cycles, coinci-
dent with diverse fantasies of the protagonist
Pilorge, bear a resemblance to the cyclic pat-
terns of the act of love: desire, paroxysm and
slump. The structural characteristics of the
poem are, in addition, ambivalent, corresponding
to parallels in the existential circumstances of
the poet and Pilorge, both of whom were incarcerated and possibly both amorous; the structure reflects an ambiguity of optic and of voice. The
statement "En esprit je revis avec lui" implies

a degree of fusion in the identities of the poet
and his protagonist; in the actual poem, the
voice which sings in the effusive stanzas appears to be that of Pilorge, indulging in an
erotic lament for a beloved youth whose criminal
radiance and exquisite private parts will no
longer lighten his own numbered days. Since
Pilorge is dead, it is clearly not Pilorge who
sings; more likely it is an aspect of Genet who,
the dedication tells us, loved Pilorge; who la-
ments him even as the poem affirms the splendour
of his death. Thus one may discern an ambivalence in those parts of the work which apply as
much to "Genet" as to the condemned man. Since
Pilorge is moreover "Genet's" creation, his
creature, he is in a sense his prisoner; Pilorge
is held within the poem as "Genet" is held within
his cell. The protagonist's fantasies uncurl
within an implicitly dual projection.

Each movement is initiated by mention of
some banal phenomenon linked with prison life
which, impinging on the consciousness of the condemned man, triggers associations that soon develop into wild erotic fantasy. Thus, at the
poem's inception, the poet explores some rather
trite images - Sartre has compared them to the
worst of François Coppée - to introduce by simulated association the image of the gorgeous
youth:

> Un pauvre oiseau qui meurt et le
>   goût de la cendre,
> Le souvenir d'un oeil endormi sur
>   le mur,
> Et ce poing douloureux qui menace
>   l'azur,
> Font au creux de ma main ton
>   visage descendre.
>   (Poèmes, p. 9)

Each fantasy has as its subject this adored boy,
whom the condemned man pictures in a series of
erotically appetising postures and impostures,
and for whom he imagines a similar career in
crime, with attendant pederastic triumphs. In

the first lyrical division, the youth becomes
among other things a cabin boy, exciting not
merely to Pilorge in his revery but also to a
group of tough sailors enclosed within that
fantasy:

> Et c'est pour t'emmancher, beau
>   mousse d'aventure,
> Qu'ils bandent sous leur froc les
>   matelots musclés.
> Mon amour, mon amour, voleras-tu
>   les clés
> Qui m'ouvriront le ciel où tremble
>   la mâture
>
> D'où tu sèmes royal les blancs
>   enchantements,
> Ces neiges sur mon page, en ma
>   prison muette.
> L'épouvante, les morts dans les
>   fleurs de violette
> La mort avec ses coqs! Ses
>   fantômes d'amants!
>   (Poèmes, p. 11)

Sailors and things maritime are frequently endowed with erotic connotations in Genet's literary universe, and in this instance the ship's
mast provides a ready if obvious symbol for the
beloved boy's member, the seminal snows of which
appall the condemned man since they are immediately transformed into metaphorical harbingers of
death. The pattern is repeated throughout the
poem; as the sexual tension of each revery mounts,
so does the vital anguish of the moribund man,
the poetic expression of each erotic climax coinciding with an explosion of mortal despair.
A period of relative calm then ensues before each
lyrical movement - the first one includes two
such paroxysms - ends with a return to the circumstantial reality of the prisoner's cell:

> Les matins solennels, le rhum,
>   la cigarette...
> Les ombres du tabac, du bagne et
>   des marins

> Visitent ma cellule où me roule
> et m'étreint
> Le spectre d'un tueur à la lourde
> braguette.
> (Poèmes, p. 14)

This quatrain, which concludes the first group of stanzas, also serves to illustrate the poem's ambivalence, since the man haunted by the phantasmal assassin could as well be the poet as Pilorge.

Related to the thematic development of Le Condamné is Genet's elaboration of private myths. This process resembles the simulated associations of the poem's beginning, but is more vigorous in its justification of seemingly gratuitous apparitions. Genet's mythological tendencies assume two principal forms in this work: there are places, and there are persons. In the former category may be set the erotic marine paradise, suggested in the cabin-boy interlude but not fully developed. This is in turn related to the principal erotic paradise of remote French Guiana, the legendary "bagne" or life-long preventive detention camp to which most of Genet's French-interned convicts would seem to aspire:

> On dit que la Guyane est une terre
> chaude.
>
> O la douceur du bagne impossible
> et lointain!
> O le ciel de la Belle, ô la mer
> et les palmes,
> Les matins transparents, les soirs
> fous, les nuits calmes,
> O les cheveux tondus et les
> Peaux-de-satin.
> (Poèmes, p. 12)

Guiana may be termed the equivalent, in Le Condamné à mort, of the refrain "luxe, calme et volupté" of l'Invitation au voyage. This distant unattainable territory, which represents an

oneiric release from the grisly reality of the
death cell, is presently peopled with eminently
attractive figures of the condemned man's
imagining:

> Rêvons ensemble, Amour, à quelque
>   dur amant
> Grand comme l'univers mais le corps
>   taché d'ombres.
> Il nous bouclera nus dans ces
>   auberges sombres,
> Entre ses cuisses d'or, sur son
>   ventre fumant,
>
> Un mac ébouissant taillé dans un
>   archange
> Bandant sur les bouquets d'oeillets
>   et de jasmins...
>   (Poèmes, p. 12)

The mythical presentation of this enormous ideal
lover has overtones that are biblical; Pilorge
being in erotic paradise, it is logical for the
poet to forge the myth of the dominating sexual
archangel, or superpimp. Guiana is also the
scene for an odd nuptial rite in one of the terminal fantasies, in which appears the adolescent
later identified as Bulkaen:

> Dressé seul au-dessus des rigides
>   fougères
> Le plus jeune est posé sur ses hanches
>   légères
> Immobile, attendant d'être sacré
>   l'époux.
>   (Poèmes, p. 21)

The tenderness that Pilorge feels for the youth
receives the nearest thing to consummation in
this their imaginary wedding in Guiana.

Linked with the mythical projection of
the young lover's murderous future is the quasi-
apocalyptic apparition of the iron rider:

> Toi quand tu seras prêt, en arme
>   pour le crime,

> Masqué de cruauté, casqué de cheveux
> blonds...
>
> Apparaitra sur terre un chevalier
> de fer
> Impassible et cruel, visible malgré
> l'heure
> Dans le geste imprécis d'une vieille
> qui pleure.
> (<u>Poèmes</u>, p. 15)

The apparition of the horseman has erotic connotations in that the rigidity of iron corresponds
to certain steely qualities of the erect male
member. There is furthermore a thematic connection between the nocturnal vigil of the novice
knight in chivalric myth, the watch kept with
the man condemned to die at dawn, and the trial
to be endured by the novice assassin:

> Chaque fête du sang délègue un
> beau garçon
> Pour soutenir l'enfant dans sa
> première épreuve.
> (<u>Poèmes</u>, p. 16)

The metallic phenomenon is thus far from gratuitous.

So far I have discussed in a general way
the themes and architecture of the poems, without
more specific reference to individual words and
grammatical structures. As Sartre has remarked,
two quatrains of identical grammatical construction - three clauses qualifying nouns, a causative
"font" at the end of each stanza - open the poem,
with the function of introducing the adolescent
object of the prisoner's revery:

> Le vent qui roule un coeur...
> Un ange qui sanglote...
> La colonne d'azur qu'entortille le
> marbre...
> Font ouvrir dans ma nuit...
>
> Un pauvre oiseau qui meurt...
> Le souvenir d'un oeil...

```
...ce poing qui menace...
Font au creux de ma main ton visage
    descendre.
```

The following two quatrains describe the adolescent's face, by means of a rather pedestrian present tense:

```
Ce visage...
        ...est noyé de pleurs.
Il est sombre et féroce...
Ton visage est sévère: il est d'un
    pâtre grec...
```

In the fifth quatrain, however, a series of grammatically awkward questions terminates in an essential verb, to sing:

```
Quel haut mal l'a fondu si ton
    visage chante?
```

In succeeding quatrains imperative and interrogative verb forms introduce the various fantasies and enable the poem to proceed:

```
Gamin d'or sois plutôt princesse
    d'une tour,
Rêvant mélancholique à notre pauvre
    amour...
Mon Amour, mon Amour, voleras-tu les
    clefs...
Rêvons ensemble, Amour, à quelque
    dur amant...
```

Of the verbs employed, "to sing" returns significantly often, sometimes imperatively, sometimes descriptively, furthering the illusion of a "chant" extracted from the imaginary lover:

```
Ne chante pas ce soir les
    "Costauds de la lune"...
Il descend vers le soir pour
    chanter sur le pont...
Gamin, ne chantez pas...
            (Poèmes, pp. 10-12)
```

Occasionally the viewpoint changes, complicating
the optical ambivalence of the whole; Pilorge
imagines himself singing to the youth, explicitly
and within the framework of the poem:

> ....Ecoute, il te raconte,
> Ton amant l'assassin, sa geste en
>   mille éclats
>
> Il chante qu'il avait ton corps
>   et ton visage...

The motif of the song recurs throughout the poem;
melodious snatches, both figurative and literal,
are wafted to and fro in the condemned man's cell
like eternal but ephemeral essences of criminal
masculinity:

> La chanson qui traverse un monde
>   ténébreux
> C'est le cri d'un marlou porté par
>   ta musique,
> C'est le chant d'un pendu raidi
>   comme une trique
> C'est l'appel enchanté d'un
>   voleur amoureux.
>   (Poèmes, p. 14)

Since the notions of song and poetry have evident
connections, the "chant" justifies the lyric
stanzas, becoming a natural artifice by which
the poem lives. Le Condamné might be termed,
ponderously it is true, the song of the song of
Pilorge; once again, circular and double.

"Résumés, les poèmes lyriques se réduisent
aux signifiés Amour et Mort," writes Roland
Barthes, evidently conscious of the drastic nature
of this reduction.[9] Le Condamné, apparently no
exception, joins these two "signifiés" in a particularly violent manner, since the song of
Pilorge concerns both his violent crime and his
erotic anguish at approaching violent death. For
love, and somewhat more romantically than in the
dedication, Pilorge kills an unknown female
rival:

J'ai tué pour les yeux bleus d'un
    bel indifférent
Qui jamais ne comprit mon amour
    contenue,
Dans sa gondole noire une amante
    inconnue,
Belle comme un navire et morte en
    m'adorant.
                        (Poèmes, p. 15)

Each of his erotic fantasies erupts with a simultaneous crisis of tenderness and bitterness at
his imminent decease. When finally in defiance
and revolt Pilorge invokes the souls of his vic-
tims, it is to project a sinister notion of his
murderous artistry and of its violent consummation:

Ames de mes tués! Tuez-moi!
    Brûlez-moi!
Michel-Ange exténué, j'ai taillé
    dans la vie
Mais la beauté, Seigneur, toujours
    je l'ai servie...
Messieurs je n'ai pas peur! Si ma
    tête roulait
Dans le son du panier avec ta tête
    blanche,
La mienne par bonheur sur ta
    gracile hanche
Ou pour plus de beauté, sur ton
    cou mon poulet...
                        (Poèmes, p. 23-24)

In this confusion of vital members one may perceive the expression of an ancient literary theme,
according to which love and death are one and
the same thing. One thinks, in this connection,
of the sixteenth-century English connotation of
the verb "to die." Jean Genet is clearly not
Ronsard, nor is he quite a Romantic, although
this imaginary twin decapitation of Pilorge and
his lover does resemble a passage of Flaubert:

    J'aurai pu être attaché à la colonne

près de la tienne, face à face,
sour tes yeux, répondant à tes cris
par mes soupirs; et nos douleurs se
seraient confondues, nos âmes se
seraient mêlées. (Il se flagèle
avec furie.) Tiens, tiens, Pour toi
encore! [10]

As in each of the cyclic fantasies, the exaltation is accompanied by bitterness and followed
by a lull; in this case it is also succeeded by
some rather sentimental stanzas apostrophizing
God, one of which contains a blunt return to
reality and the dissolution of the poem:

> Ce n'est pas ce matin que l'on me
>   guillotine.
> Je peux dormir tranquille. A l'étage
>   au-dessus
> Mon mignon paresseux, ma perle, mon
>   Jésus
> S'éveille. Il va cogner de sa dure
>   bottine
> A mon crâne tendu.
>   (Poèmes, p. 26)

Le Condamné à mort invites an immediate
but brief comparison with Oscar Wilde's Ballad
of Reading Gaol, a somewhat lugubrious penal reminiscence to which it is generically related.
Wilde's poem, which is composed around the theme
of "Each man kills the thing he loves," is dedicated to the memory of a former guardsman,
apparently hanged in Reading prison on July 7,
1896 for the murder of his mistress. Both poems
involve meditations on the nature of capital
punishment, both were written in memory of men
who killed their lovers, and in both works the
poet observes a nocturnal vigil:

> The warders with their shoes of felt
>   Crept by each padlocked door,
> And peeped and saw, with eyes of awe,
>   Grey figures on the floor,
> And wondered why men knelt to pray
>   Who never prayed before. [11]

The two poems differ vastly, however, in that
Le Condamné is specifically and unmitigatedly
pederastic in theme and graphically erotic in
its visual appeal, whereas the Ballad is completely bereft of such elements. Unlike Genet,
Wilde the poet-prisoner surveys his protagonist
from a sympathetic and horrified distance, treating in emotional terms of man's dreadful inhu-
manity to man and uttering a Christian plea
against the gallows. Genet, on the other hand,
is bent on demonstrating the innate and irresistible splendour of the soul of one Pilorge, and
on poetically justifying the manner of his
death.

　　　　Unlike Le Condamné and the novel Notre-
Dame-des-Fleurs, Marche funèbre bears no actual
dedication to Maurice Pilorge whose presence nonetheless pervades the work. Genet's second published poem appeared with Le Condamné in Marc
Barbezat's 1945 edition of Chants secrets. It is
useful to recall that according to the dedication
of the earlier poem Pilorge had received a double
sentence, being condemned both to life imprisonment and to the guillotine, a circumstance to
which no doubt pertain both works' twin preoccupations with execution and prolonged incarceration.

　　　　Despite evident similarities of theme,
the two poems differ in both form and content.
Whereas Le Condamé à mort comprises seventy or
so quatrains with practically no metric variation,
Marche funèbre boasts of four species of stanza
and thirteen lyrical divisions of varying dura-
tion. Furthermore, the initial viewpoint of the
poet has changed in that Genet appears to consider the obsessive Pilorge objectively, that is,
from without; it is no longer Pilorge who de-
claims, but the imprisoned poet. That sleep,
dreams and the sub-conscious are emphasised in
this work may even be deemed indicative of a desire to objectify and thus possess the cause of
the obsession. At several junctures, however,
the poet seems once again to be assimilated with

Pilorge, to the point where he dreams of that beheaded soul inhabiting his own body. Genet's
principal theme remains the apotheosis of the
dead assassin, complicated in this second poem
by a rudimentary psychiatric mysticism and a
growing literary self-consciousness which causes
him to view his poetic endeavours as the eventual
subject of the poem itself. These themes are
further embroiled by a series of oppositions one
would like to term dialectic, were they less confused, contrasting night and day, nudity and
vesture, acts and immobility. Also present are
a bevy of black warriors, angels, white bodies
and decapitated roses.

The poem's movements are too numerous
and varied to permit of detailed analysis of
each; I shall therefore briefly indicate the
manner in which the interwoven themes are expanded. The first two stanzas of the poem establish a nocturnal setting and inform us that the
poet suffers in his cell from a sleep made
treacherous by dreams, thereby hinting at those
workings of the sub-conscious which will develop
into a major theme:

> Perfide est le sommeil où la
> prison m'emporte
> Et plus obscurément dans mes
> couloirs secrets...
> (_Poèmes_, p. 31)

It soon becomes apparent that the poet is haunted
by the somnambulistic emanations of a criminal
boy, later to be identified as Pilorge. The
cause of the obsession is primarily represented
in the thrice-repeated metaphor of amorous confinement:

> C'est en moi qu'il me boucle et
> jusqu'à perpète
> Ce gâfe de vingt ans!
> Un seul geste son oeil, ses cheveux
> dans ses dents:
> Mon coeur s'ouvre et le gaffe avec un
> cri de fête
> M'emprisonne dedans.
> (_Poèmes_, p. 33)

The circumstantial parallel which effects the
occasional ambiguities of Le Condamné à mort is
thus inverted; the poet-prisoner's protagonist,
trapped upon his page, now metaphorically incar-
cerates his creator. The word "obsession" itself, used here to designate this essential theme,
and which may refer to preoccupations both conscious and unconscious, seems particularly apposite if one ponders its derivation: obsidere,
to besiege. Related to the notions of sleep and
obsession are some odd somnolent communions of
poet and lover in the poem's third division.

Despite the metric variations evident in
the opening movements of Marche funèbre, all
three stanza forms contain the alexandrine as a
basic unit. In the poem's fourth movement, however, a change of theme coincides with an abrupt
alteration of form. There results a rhythmic
condensation reminiscent of Valéry:

> Belles nuits du plein jour
> Ténèbres de Pilorge
> C'est dans vos noirs détours
> Mon couteau que l'on forge.
>   (Poèmes, p. 34)

Paradox by definition implies a conflict of
meanings; it is this faintly manichean opposition of day and night, resolved by an intensity
of passion into blazing oxymoronic darkness,
that prepares the notion of the wicked angel, a
conceit appropriate both to Pilorge and the poet.
As befits the private mythology of an erotic
supernatural, an angel, disembodied but visually
incarnate, can float through prison walls much
as a beauteous boy can haunt the labyrinthine
corridors of mind. Genet further chooses the
Luciferian metaphor of fall to express an awareness of aesthetic error, committed generally in
seeking to celebrate things other than the angelic
youth:

> Quand j'ai voulu chanter d'autres
>   gammes que lui
> Ma plume s'embrouillant dans les
>   rais de lumière

> D'un mot vertigineux la tête la
>   première
> Stupide je tombais par cette erreur
>   conduit
> Au fond de son ornière.
>   (Poèmes, p. 36)

The wicked angel is thus connected with both the
poet's romantic obsession and the dawning of his
artistic consciousness.

That the celebration of Maurice Pilorge
involves recognition of his dual sentence helps
to account for various oppositions of deed and
immobility which occur in the poem, connected
rather obviously with the opposition of life and
death:

> L'eau de la solitude
> Immobile me garde et remplit la prison.
> J'ai vingt ans pour toujours et malgré
>   votre étude.
>
> Pour te plaire ô gamin d'une sourde
>   beauté
> Je resterai vêtu jusqu'à ce que je
>   meure
> Et ton âme quittant ton corps décapité
> Trouvera dans mon corps une blanche
>   demeure.
>   (Poèmes, p. 36)

The poet's desire to be assimilated with Pilorge,
interminably interned and simultaneously executed
for his twenty years, is thus once again linked
with the topic of decapitation. Execution may
be termed an act inasmuch as it involves an agent
and effects a transition into death; and thus the
assassin's violent demise contrasts with the mo-
tionless nature of his life imprisonment. As in
Le Condamné, however, the celebration's bloody
culmination is complicated by strong erotic overtones:

> Malgré les soldats noirs qui bais-
>   seront leurs lances

Tu ne peux fuir du lit où le
    masque de fer
T'immobilise raide et soudain tu
    t'élances
Retombes sans bouger et reviens
    en enfer.
                            (Poèmes, p. 41)

The medieval and heavily phallic connotations of
the iron horseman in Le Condamné are redoubled in
these images of male rigidity and enforced fatal
sexual spasm; Pilorge in apotheosis is depicted
at a moment of convulsion and eternal immobility.
Further morbid adornment is provided by the
symbol of the rose:

    ...Il signera Pilorge et son
        apothéose
    Sera l'échafaud clair d'où
        jaillissent les roses
        Bel effet de la mort.
                            (Poèmes, p. 43)

The sanguinary connection between spurting blood
and roses is clear and will recur in Miracle de
la Rose and La Galère, in which the truncated
blooms personnify and represent the destiny of
the dead killer Harcamone. In view of the court-
ly tradition that associates roses with a lady's
intimate favours, it is tempting to infer notions
of castration, since that which is cut off in
such instances effectively disqualifies the victim from erotic pursuits. [12] In both Le Condamné
and Marche funèbre one is reminded that in France
the sexual act is sometimes called "La petite
mort," a term which Genet uses nowhere, but which
alludes conveniently to the biological similarities of death and orgasm. In both poems the need
to counteract mortality would seem to explain
the extension of desire or amorous revery.

        The essential themes of prison, erotic
obsession and celebration are all related to the
theme of poetic creation, which emerges as the
final subject of the poem. The origin and focal

point of many themes is the prison itself. Apos-
trophising his beloved dingy cell the poet dis-
covers therein a correlative to his own mental
processes:

> Tes couloirs ténébreux sont méandres
>   du coeur
> Et leur masse de rêve organise en
>   silence
> Un mécanisme ayant du vers la
>   ressemblance
> Et l'exacte rigueur.
>   (Poèmes, p. 41)

A nocturnal fluid flowing in the cell, suggestive
of a writer's ink, the "eau de la solitude," and,
if one wishes, Styx and Lethe, is readily identi-
fiable as darkness, but links by liquid reminiscence several minor themes. In a somewhat clumsy
burst of poetic self-criticism, the poet attributes to a "complexual obsession" with death other
recurrent images:

> Le hasard fit sortir - le plus
>   grand! des hasards
> Trop souvent de ma plume au coeur
>   de mes poèmes
> La rose avec le mot de Mort qu'à
>   leurs brassards
> En blanc portent brodé les noirs
>   guerriers que j'aime.
>   (Poèmes, p. 43)

Naively psychiatric, the poet decides that by indulging his preoccupations with the mortal muse
he will re-discover a phallic figure of his childhood, "l'étranger à la verge fleurie," thereby
investing his creation with further mystery even
as it purports to shrug off its obsessive shroud.
Marche funèbre ends with a self-conscious image of
the poet-prisoner bent over his discouraging
travail and entering into an unexpected complicity
with the reader:

> Si vous pouviez me voir sur ma
>   table penché

Le visage défait par ma propre
littérature...
(Poèmes, p. 47)

The ironic inversion of the creative mind thus
reflecting on itself constitutes a terminal modi-
fication of the poem's constant duality, a duality perceptible both in the paradoxical oppositions of themes and in permutations in the parallel circumstances of the poet and his creature
Pilorge.

(c) La Galère

La Galère would seem to have been composed some time before the novel Miracle de la
Rose of which it may be said to anticipate a
segment. This third minor work was first published as a collector's item by Jacques Loyau in
1947, with elegant erotic illustrations by
Leonor Fini;[13] stripped of its graphic embellishments, it reappeared with the other poems in
the Marc Barbezat edition of 1948. The manner
of its composition has been recorded and com-
mented upon by Sartre: "Vers ce temps-là,
j'avais écrit deux poèmes sans qu'ils aient de
rapport l'un avec l'autre. Je les ai mélangés,
pensant donner plus d'obscurité, plus de densité
à mes vers."[14] Genet's own reiterated words
serve to indicate the critical problems posed by
this refractory variation of his dualistic
tendencies.

The title of this fresh eruption of
alexandrines evokes one of those flat, oared
vessels in which criminals or slaves, frequently
in chains, were formerly despatched to die in
distant climes. The grisly theme appealed to
the Romantics; Jean Valjean did time aboard a
galley; Turner, in his stunning and controversial
Slave Ship, and Heinrich Heine, in a violently
satirical ballad, depicted in their different
ways the iniquities of the slave trade. Genet's

poem, however, has only the most tenuous connections with social criticism and the nineteenth-
century colourists. In his fantasy the galley
becomes an oneiric instrument of libidinous liberation on which the convicts, presumably bound
for Guiana and preventive incarceration, revolt
and sodomise each other unrestrainedly. An orgy
of olympian proportions is presided over in spirit
by Harcamone, another decapitated murderer who
will reappear in Miracle de la Rose mystically
betrothed to the narrator. The galley of the
title, therefore, has twin functions that pertain
to the fantastic and the real. A vehicle of
escape, it is also to some extent an imaginative
instrument of quest, by which the poet seeks out
his erotic monarch Harcamone.

Maritime and penal themes, tinged with
eroticism and revolt, emerge even from the poem's
opening lines, in which complex images are suggested by curiously intermingled meanings:

> Un forçat délivré dur et féroce
>   lance
> Un chiourme dans le pré mais d'une
>   fleur de lance
> Le marlou Croix du Sud l'assassin
>   Pôle Nord
> Aux oreilles d'un autre ôtent ses
>   boucles d'or
> Les plus beaux sont fleuris d'étranges
>   maladies.
> Leur croupe de guitare éclate en
>   mélodies.
> L'écume de la mer nous mouille de
>   crachats.
>   (Poèmes, p. 51)

Preliminary ambiguities are concentrated in the
first two lines, which convey a rather odd impression if "lancer" is taken in its usual sense of
"throw;" more plausible in this context would be
an erotic reading, since the phallic lance recalls
"l'étranger à la verge fleurie." One is also reminded that in argot "le grand pré" is synonymous

with "bagne." The nautical resonances emitted
by the pseudonyms are echoed in the reference to
spray, a form of fluid which will become virtually interchangeable with tears and seminal emissions in the course of the poem. The notion of
the secret femininity of criminals suggested in
these lines by mentions of earrings and musical
rumps, prepares the apparition of Harcamone, who
flies into the poem in feminine guise:

> Harcamone aux bras verts haute
>   reine qui vole
> Sur ton odeur nocturne et les
>   bois éveillés
> Par l'horreur de son nom ce
>   bagnard endeuillé
> Sur ma galère chante et son chant
>   me désole.
>   (Poèmes, p. 51)

As in Le Condamné, the pretext of song justifies
the poem, in this case linking Harcamone with the
slave-galley, thus with the poet's imaginary
voyage.

In the ensuing lines the olfactory sense
dominates, adding to Harcamone's nocturnal odour
such related elements as farts and the melodious
bottoms, wine and the azure sky, roses and the
elusive doe. In its fragile unpredictability
this latter animal comes to symbolise the tempera-
mental male member, and is thus intimately linked
with the theme of escape:

> Pourtant la biche est prise à son
>   piège de feuille
> Dans l'aurore elle égoutte un adieu
>   transparent...
>   (Poèmes, p. 51)

Femininely delicate, the flower and the lady fawn
are metaphorically related by their habit of
hiding behind the "foliage" of fly-buttons, where
their natural vulnerability is contrasted with
evocations of rigidity:

```
    Tiges à pleines mains corolles
          se redressent
    Corolles sont de plume et les
          membres de plomb
               (Poèmes, p. 59)
```

Erection, an essential part of male erotic release, is achieved in spectacular wise aboard the
poet's anthropomorphic vessel. As in Le Condamné,
the invention of a cabin-boy provides stimulus:

```
    Ils le vêtent d'écume et d'algues
          de velours.
    L'amour faisant valser leur bite
          enturbannée
    (Biche bridant l'azur et rose
          boutonnée)
    Les cordes et les corps étaient
          raides de noeuds.
    Et bandait la galère.  Un mot
          vertigineux
    Venu du fond du monde abolit le
          bel ordre.
               (Poèmes, p. 54)
```

In the course of the orgy, and consequently of
the poem, the success of these sodomitic frolics
is measured in terms of the ship's withdrawal
from France, and of the poet's pursuit of the
doe. As might be expected, the desire for liberation and the erotic quest for Harcamone culminate
in the successive tumescences of poet and
assassin:

```
    Dans un bosquet charmant où cette
          biche pleure
    Un être de la nuit dont le froc
          paresseux
    Baissa le pont de toile à mon
          libre vaisseau.
    La rose d'eau se ferme au bord de
          ma main bleue.
    ...Sur le ciel tu t'épands Harcamone!
          et froissé
    Le ciel s'est couvert mais d'un
          geste amusé.
               (Poèmes, p. 64)
```

45

This rather precious but apparently successful
identification of rose, doe, ship and member is
followed by a return to sadness occasioned by
the poet's inevitable awareness of Harcamone's
death:

Astres je vous dégueule et ma peine
        est pareille
Harcamone à ta main à ta main morte
        qui pend.
...Voyage sur la lune ou la mer je
        ne sais
Harcamone au cou rose entouré
        d'un lacet.
                        (Poèmes, p. 65)

The poem thus expires upon images of Harcamone
with mutilated neck floating in the moon or
drifting in the deep, the lunar alternative being
faintly reminiscent of Beardsley's illustration
for Salomé, the watery end following more in the
tradition of burial at sea.

The recurring themes of prison, escape,
erotico-maritime paradise and executed killers
would seem at first sight to link this poem with
the two preceding ones; yet La Galère differs in
the nature of its structural caprice and increased
linguistic ambiguity. That much of the poem was
intended to remain obscure, as indicated by
Genet's whimsical fusion of two unrelated works,
is suggested on a different level by the exaggerated arch preciosity with which he veils, for
example, masturbation:

Hèlas! Ma main captive est morte
        sans mourir.
Les jardins disent non où la biche
        est vêtue
D'une robe de neige et ma grâce
        la tue
Pour la mieux d'un linceul d'écume
        revêtir.
                        (Poèmes, p. 55)

Obfuscation accordingly results from peculiarities in both structure and style. Ambivalent in
its increased preciosity, La Galère further differs from its predecessors in an intensified use
of words of multiple meaning; the erotic-escapist
connotations of "la biche" would appear confirmed
by the fact that in the criminal argot of Genet's
reform school Mettray, "se bicher" is synonymous
with "s'évader."[15] Despite a number of argotic
expressions such as "mino," "gaffe" and a virtuosic selection of phallic synonyms, Le Condamné
and Marche funèbre contain scant equivocation of
the sort caused by words having two acceptable
but distinct meanings enclosed within the normal
frames of syntax. La Galère further differs in
the separation of its tenses, a division which
may possibly indicate the component parts of the
original poems; in lascivious ship-board pursuits
the narrative slips from the static present of
the prison cell into a more active imperfect,
whereas in the previous poems the fantasies un-
fold in the present or future tenses. La Galère
resembles a gigantic orgiastic fresco in which
general and individual scenes of titillation
contribute to the cumulative whole, the poet's
oneiric voyage within himself being objectified
by the past narrative tenses which present his
erotic quest as an accomplished fact.

(d) Literary Borrowings

        Although critics have written very little
about Genet's poems, they do appear to have been
struck by the quantity of evident nineteenth-
and twentieth-century borrowings. Sartre has
listed elements of Cocteau, Valéry and Verlaine,
Hugo, Baudelaire and "everyone" - in that order -
and argues that this culturally dispossessed
thief "steals" the accepted idioms of modern
poetry for his first attempts at literature. Indeed, if Genet's apocalyptic visions, elegiac
melancholy, marine fantasies seem in places to
suggest nineteenth-century "thefts," the elements

of neo-classicism and surrealism evident in his
penal poems can best be traced to Jean Cocteau.
The influence of Cocteau is suggested by the
facts of acquaintance, by Genet's (literal) theft
of his works, and by the younger poet's reportedly considering these poems too Cocteauesque. The
plethora of classical allusions resulting from
these borrowings reflects at several removes
Cocteau's interest in mythology and the supernatural aspects of Christianity. This multiplicity of influences - for one might also list
Apollinaire and the Consolation à M. du Périer
among the more amusing echos - adds a parasitic
level of duplicity to the ambivalence of structure
and optique.

      Cocteauesque elements loom larger in
Genet's first two poems than in any other work
except the virtually contemporaneous Notre-Dame-
des-Fleurs. Of these two poems, angelic trans-
plants and surrealist affinities are probably
more apparent in Marche funèbre. In Le Condamné
à mort neo-classical tendencies are superficially
manifest in allusions to two gods, the "Hermès
au tendre pied" of the concluding stanzas, and
the Pilorge-as-Apollo of the Dédicace. The identification of Pilorge with Apollo is apt; errone-
ously but traditionally associated with the sun,
Apollo was also something of a pederast, at
least in Ovid's Metamorphoses, in which he
accidentally kills fair Hyacinthus with a discus.
He is also, as Cocteau occasionally reminds the
reader, the tutelary god of poetry. Possibly
Genet found a precedent for his moribund Apollo
in Cocteau's Cherchez Apollon of 1932, a short
oracular poem in which the god dies in a fashion
both cryptic and spectacular. But the more general, diffuse manner in which Genet apparently
attempts to adapt Cocteau's personal poetic idioms
to his own not always fortunate imagery may be
illustrated by comparing the initial lines of
his Condamné à mort with those of Cocteau's
Prière mutilée:

Le vent qui roule un coeur sur le
    pavé des cours,
Un ange qui sanglote accroché dans
    un arbre,
La colonne d'azur qu'entortille le
    marbre
Font ouvrir dans ma nuit des portes
    de secours.
                (Poèmes, p. 9)

Le système du ciel se soulève,
    rameurs
Entre vos doigts tragiques
    d'Avril;
Et les anges cueillant les étoiles
    mures
Du tonnerre roulaient l'amoureux
    baril.[16]

Metaphorical animation of the elements takes
place in both quatrains, yet Genet's images remain unhappily literal, suggesting an imperfect
understanding of both the imitation and the
medium involved. The wedding of vegetable and
wretched seraph - "Un ange qui sanglote, etc."
- is reminiscent of other, single lines of
Cocteau, such as "Bel ange attendez-moi derrière
l'arbre à songe," from Conseil de toute importance. Sometimes, however, influences may be
multiple; the line "La mort avec ses coqs! Ses
fantômes d'amants!" would seem to recall not only
shades of Cocteau's insomniac poultry or ambivalent phantoms but also, in its morbidly erotic
context, Apollinaire's "Les coqs s'épuisaient en
fanfares" from Les Sept Epées.

    In Marche funèbre, the diverse influences
of Plain-Chant, certain poems of Opéra, and even
the metaphysics of La Machine infernale are in
several places evident. The nocturnal emanations
of Pilorge, for example, distinctly resemble
numerous stanzas of Plain-Chant in which the poet,
temporarily escaping from the ministrations of his

angel-muse, meditates upon the dreams that possess his sleeping lover. Thus Genet's

> Quand tu dors des chevaux déferlent
>   dans la nuit
> Sur ta poitrine plate et le galop
>   des bêtes
> Ecarte la ténèbre où le sommeil
>   conduit
> Sa puissante machine arrachée à
>   ma tête
> Et sans le moindre bruit
> Le sommeil fait fleurir de tes pieds
>   tant de branches
> Que j'ai peur de mourir étouffé par
>   leurs cris.
>   (Poèmes, pp. 32-3)

echo Cocteau's

> Cette tête coupée, allant en d'autres
>   mondes,
>   Où regne une autre loi,
> Plongeant dans le sommeil des racines
>   profondes,
> Loin de moi, près de moi.
>
> ...Mais le noeud dénoué ne laisse que
>   du vide;
>   Et tu prends le cheval aux crins,
> Le cheval du sommeil, qui, d'un sabot
>   rapide,
>   Te dépose aux bords que je crains.
>
> Tiens ton bel oeil ouvert. Veille.
>   Car je redoute
> Ce sommeil machiné qui te transporte
>   ailleurs.[17]

In both poems a fascination with sleep and dreams
and the autonomous motions of body and brain constitute a theme of surrealistic possibilities; in
both poems, the analysis of fantasy and poetic
activity are linked with, or emerge as, their own
major themes. It is probable that Cocteau's not
infrequent metaphorical equation of trees,

50

branches and roots with man's central nervous
system inspired Genet's similar appropriation
of nature's largest plant, apparent both in the
above quotation and in later segments of that
poem:

> Séchant selon mes voeux
> Je fixe le silence
> Quand les oiseaux de feu
> De mon arbre s'élancent.
> (Poèmes, p. 35)

> Sur le buisson ardent du système
>   nerveux
> Où sèche mon linge, apparut
> Un bras en l'air aux veines bleues.[18]

This same portion of Marche funèbre is also
rather similar to Cocteau's short poem Dormeurs
jouant à l'hombre, again from the collection
Opéra, in which puns to the order of hombre-
homme-ombre and amour-mourre weave onanistic
connotations into a dream-like borderline between
light and shade. More significant, however, in
its metaphysical and, subsequently, fictional
ramifications is an allusion to the criminal
destiny of Pilorge that would seem to derive
from the death of Jocaste in La Machine infernale:

> Pris au piège des dieux étranglé
>   par leur soie
> Tu es mort sans savoir ni pourquoi
>   ni comment.
> (Poèmes, p. 41)

One recalls that in Cocteau's play the queen,
having repeatedly tripped on an unmanageable
and menacing scarf, eventually hangs herself
with it. Cocteau's metaphysics of the divine
booby trap and his artistic doctrine of lying
for the greater truth are manifest in both Opéra
and La Machine infernale, yet the strangulation
by silk points, in this case, to Genet having
known the play. Traps, destiny, the hostility

of objects and the problem of fictional "truth"
are all themes that will return, more impres-
sively, in Notre-Dame-des-Fleurs.

Among the remaining literary influences
or borrowings which one might choose to discuss,
two in particular underline problems of genre
and artistic intent which might, for some readers,
constitute the poems' ultimate flaws. A curious
borrowing from Malherbe, of plainly elegiac
nature, seems almost so blatant as to destroy any
possible poignant associations:

> Le sort détruit encor par un nouveau
>   trépas
>   Nos amours désolées,
> Car c'était encor toi Pilorge ne
>   mens pas
>   Que ces ombres volées!
>   (Poèmes, p. 37)

> Le malheur de ta fille au tombeau
>   descendue
>   Par un commun trépas,
> Est-ce quelque Dédale, ou ta
>   raison perdue
>   Ne se retrouve pas...[19]

The Consolation à M. du Périer, which Genet's
poem recalls in its metrical form and in the
rhyming of "trépas...pas," is the sort of verse
that Genet might be expected to have read in some
anthology of a reform insitution library, and
its incidence in Marche funèbre is somewhat amusing. In like wise rhythm, vocabulary and a relative absence of punctuation suggest Apollinaire's
"Adieu Adieu/ Soleil cou coupé" as a source for
certain lines of Le Condamné:

>   ...Mes amours parfumées
> Adieu vont s'en aller! Adieu couilles
>   aimées!
> O sur ma voix coupée adieu chibre
>   insolent!
>   (Poèmes, p. 12)

This combination of deep mourning and anatomical
precision may strike some readers as faintly
comic, a reaction which, depending on their esti-
mation of Genet's poetic intent, might lead them
to a pejorative evaluation. Lines such as

> Vous pâlissez de honte à lire
> le poème
> Qu'inscrit l'adolescent aux gestes
> criminels...
> (Poèmes, p. 43)

suggest that the poet expects his readers to be
shocked, while other words addressed to prison
friends evince, rather, his own indifference:

> De votre amitié même et de vous
> je m'en fous.
> (Poèmes, p. 45)

Slight though such problems are, they do seem
indicative of an ambivalence in the poet's own
attitude to his intended effects, an ambivalence
which probably constitutes the poems' ultimate
flaw; those elements of humour and parody which
undoubtedly exist in Genet's writings can be
seen to far better advantage in the novel Notre-
Dame-des-Fleurs.

NOTES TO CHAPTER I

[1]Richard N. Coe, The Vision of Jean Genet
(New York: The Grove Press, 1968), p. 67.

[2]Roger Blin, private interview, Paris, July 19,
1972.

[3]Jean-Paul Sartre has provided the following information as to the dating of Genet's poems:
"La plupart de ses autres poèmes sont
contemporains de La Galère, c'est-à-
dire antérieurs au Miracle de la Rose
et à toutes ses grandes oeuvres. Seul
le Pêcheur du Suquet est relativement
récent.(45)"
Saint-Genet, Paris: Gallimard, 1970, p. 496.

[4]Saint-Genet, p. 474.

[5]Jean Genet, Journal du voleur (Paris:
Gallimard, 1968), p. 51.

[6]Miracle de la Rose, Oeuvres Complètes de Jean
Genet (Paris: Gallimard, 1967), II, 312.

[7]Saint-Genet, p. 416.

[8]Jean Genet, Poèmes (Lyon: Barbezat, 1966), p.
27. Subsequent references to this edition
will appear in the text.

[9]Roland Barthes, "Analyse structurale des récits,"
in Poétique du récit (Paris: Seuil, 1977),
p. 49.

[10]Flaubert, La Tentation de Saint-Antoine,
quoted by Mario Praz in his The Romantic Agony
(New York: Meridian, 1968), p. 33.

54

[11]Oscar Wilde, The Ballad of Reading Gaol, in
The Portable Oscar Wilde (New York: Viking
Press, 1967), p. 597.

[12]This suggestion is not wholly fanciful: "La
potence comme la guillotine...elles ont toujours
été la veuve du condamné - le jargon de 1628
appelait déjà ainsi la potence, - et la bourreau
est dès lors normalement le marieux, le cocu
de la veuve, l'accordeur ou le mec de la
camarade, le perruquier de la sérieuse..."
which terminology would seem to connote a
castrating widow. See Jean Graven, L'Argot
et le tatouage des criminels (Neuchâtel:
Editions de la Baconnière, 1962), p. 23.

[13]The luxurious first edition bears the following
legend:

L'EDITION ORIGINALE
DE LA GALERE, POEME DE MONSIEUR JEAN GENET,
A ETE ETABLIE PAR JACQUES LOYAU, LIBRAIRIE A
PARIS, PASSAGE DES PANORAMAS, ET IMPRIMEE
SUR LES PRESSES DE L'HOTEL DE SAGONNE, EN
JUILLET MCMXLVII, AUX FRAIS DE L'AUTEUR.

The drawings of Madame Fini, which do not contribute a great deal towards a comprehension
of the poem, depict a series of splendidly
muscular young men sprawling in groups of
twos and threes on undefined beds, pursuing
each other amorously, or standing singly in
postures of an outrageous and flirtatious
elegance.

[14]Saint-Genet, p. 495.

[15]Compare with this extract from l'Enfant criminel,
a text for a radio talk never broadcast about
reform schools:
"A Saint-Hilaire, l'un d'eux (i.e.
delinquent boys) que j'avais apprivoisé
me dit un jour:

'Quand je vous ai dit que le copain
s'était sauvé, ne répétez pas au
directeur que j'ai dit qu'il s'était
biché.'
Il avait lâché le mot. C'est celui même
que nous employions à Mettray pour
parler du gosse qui s'évade, se sauve,
courre (sic) dans les bois comme une
biche."
Jean Genet, L'Enfant criminel (Paris: Paul
Morihien, 1948), pp. 7-33.

[16]Cocteau, Opéra (Paris: Dutilleul, 1959),
unpaginated edition.

[17]Cocteau, Poèmes 1916-1955 (Paris: Gallimard,
1956).

[18]Cocteau, Opéra, unpaginated.

[19]Malherbe, François, in Les Cent Meilleurs
Poèmes Lyriques (de la langue française), ed.
August Dorchin. (Imprimé en Angleterre: House
of Grant, 24e. éd., 1957), p. 36. Conceivably,
an anthology for prison libraries.

CHAPTER II: THE NOVELIST: <u>NOTRE-DAME DES-FLEURS</u>

(a) Genesis

　　　The manner in which Genet composed the
extraordinary prose work Notre-Dame-des Fleurs,
was, once again, first recounted by Sartre, and
has accordingly entered into Genet's literary
legend. Written in prison, in pencil, on the
lumpy brown paper issued to convicts for the
fabrication of bags, the manuscript was discovered
one day by a guard who promptly burnt its extant
fifty pages. Genet began again. The whole,
which he completed in this unpropitious circumstance, is dated Fresnes 1942, and refers to
incarceration in both that institution and La
Santé; like the preceding Condamné à mort, the
work is dedicated to the memory of Maurice
Pilorge. Although a fragment and an anonymous
luxury edition appeared in 1944,[1] Notre-Dame did
not achieve commercial status until 1951, when
Gallimard began to bring out Genet's Oeuvres
Complètes. In the winter of 1976 it appeared
in the paperback collection Folio. It is frequently considered Genet's masterpiece: "Our
Lady of the Flowers," writes Lionel Abel, upon
its translated release in 1963, "...certainly a
masterpiece - the greatest novel, I should say,
since Faulkner was great - is also the book of
Genet which best reveals his style of thinking."[2]

　　　As is the case with Le Condamné à mort,
accounts of the genesis of Notre-Dame-des-Fleurs
are pertinent to its comprehension in as much as
they reveal parallels affecting the structure of
the work. These parallels are suggested in the
novel's opening pages, where an incarcerated
narrator Jean - who should not be confused with
the real Jean Genet - lists the select group of
profligates whose gross misdeeds, he claims,
inspire the book: Weidmann, Ange Soleil, Maurice
Pilorge and an unnamed naval lieutenant who has
committed treason. The isolated Jean, it transpires, has decorated his wall with their photographs, excised from a few rare mutilated journals
which somehow reach his cell:

25

> Un peu plus tôt, le nègre Ange
> Soleil avait tué sa maitresse.
>
> Un peu plus tard, le soldat
> Maurice Pilorge assassinait son amant
> Escudero pour lui voler un peu moins
> de mille francs, puis on lui coupait
> le cou pour l'anniversaire de ses
> vingt ans, alors, vous vous le rap-
> pelez, qu'il esquissait un pied de
> nez au bourreau rageur.
>
> Enfin, un enseigne de vaisseau,
> encore enfant, trahissait pour trahir:
> on le fusilla. Et c'est en l'honneur
> de leurs crimes que j'écris mon livre.
>
> Cette merveilleuse éclosion de belles
> et sombres fleurs, je ne l'ai appris
> que par fragments...[3]

Thus, the reader of this dual beginning is privy
to an autogenesis, or fictional account of the
birth of a secondary fiction; he has read both
the inception of the text Notre-Dame-des-Fleurs
and the narrator's declared intention to compose
a book. This duplicity marks the ensuing narrative in all its major aspects: structure, time,
narrative optique and "self-conscious" creation
of characters. Most notably, Pilorge finds an
equivalent or "double" in Adrien Baillon, the
titular "Notre-Dame-des-Fleurs;" both are blond,
utterly delinquent, and cut off in extreme
youth. Baillon's pseudonym, bestowed upon him
by the pimps, prostitutes and petty thieves of
nether Montmartre, is emblematic of the secret
compatibility of convicts and flowers; his crime
- the strangulation of a faded closet queen -
will perfect within Jean's secondary fiction those
criminal blossomings, "cette merveilleuse éclosion
de belles et sombre fleurs," with which the novel
Notre-Dame begins.

The heroine of the secondary fiction is
not, however, Notre-Dame-des-Fleurs but Divine-
la-Cascadeuse, a talented tapette whose chronicle

of passions and fatalities constitutes the sub-
stance of the book. Divine is always designated
in the feminine, as befits her state of mental
travesty. Her story, as presented by the narrating "Jean Genet," appears as an imponderable
blend of song and choreography - "la Divine-Saga
devrait être mimée, dansée, avec de subtiles
indications". (O.C.II., p. 23-4) It encompasses
both Divine's existence as an outrageous prostitute of the Pigalle-Blanche, and portions of her
childhood, when she was but a sensitive small boy
rejoicing in the farcically appropriate name of
Louis Culafroy. Divine's principal lover is an
eternally resplendent pimp, Mignon-les-Petits-
Pieds, who unwittingly begets the assassin Notre-
Dame-des-Fleurs. A major part of the secondary
narrative concerns Divine's "poetic" influence
on these characters in their relentless grind
towards catastrophe. Since the book's creations
are largely presented through her eyes, Divine
may be said to perform the invisible functions
of a secondary narrator, enclosed within the
framework of "Jean Genet's" primary imaginings.
Notre-Dame-des-Fleurs is thus structured by a
frame whose embedded narrative recounts the fictional destiny of Divine, while the frame itself
contains the narrator in his purportedly fictional state of awaiting judgement in a cell.
The inner and outer structures frequently con-
verge as Jean interrupts the inner narrative to
comment on the act of composition: lucid in the
control of his fiction, he effects a paradoxical
inversion of his own uncontrollable condition.

(b) Structure and Time

        The novel is initiated by five or so pre-
lusive pages roughly analagous in theme to the
posterior Dédicace of the Condamné à mort; dominated by reference to the newspaper cuttings from
which Jean extracts his own literary intent, they
justify and engender his "inner" or secondary
creative endeavour. Newspaper photographs, them-

61

selves framed and multiple - additionally framed
by little wreath-like borders of glass beads Jean
fashions in his cell - suggest an immediate visual
equivalent to the "frame" of the book itself.
This introductory segment finds a formal complement in Jean's meditation at the novel's close,
these two sections constituting the most evident
attributes of the primary, framing narrative.

That the photograph, framed and excised,
functions both as structural metaphor and structural motif appears from the opening sentence,
where reference to an evening paper forthwith
involves the reader in a legendary but banal act
of duplication:

> Weidmann vous apparut dans une
> édition de cinq heures, la tête
> emmaillotée de bandelettes blanches,
> religieuse et encore aviateur blessé,
> tombé dans des seigles, un jour de
> septembre pareil à celui où fut connu
> le nom de Notre-Dame-des-Fleurs. Son
> beau visage multiplié par les machines
> s'abattit sur Paris et sur la France,
> au plus profond des villages perdus,
> dans les châteaux et les chaumières,
> révélant aux bourgeois attristés que
> leur vie quotidienne est frôlée
> d'assassins enchanteurs...
> (O.C. II, p. 9)

The "vous" itself is double: an artifice, an
apostrophe which happens to be read by the real
reader while establishing a reader of Genet's
creation, present in the text. The image
"religieuse et encore aviateur blessé," characteristically ambivalent, anticipates in embryo
the themes of travesty and decapitation, Weidmann
being effectively beheaded by both the instru-
ments of printing and the guillotine; by analogous processes the "handsome face multiplied by
machines" is brought before the readers of,
perhaps, France-Soir, and the readers of the
novel. A critic of Genet has objected that the

real, original newspaper photograph of Weidmann
is small and difficult to see;[4] but this only
reinforces the hypothesis of fiction. Himself
a function of the novel, "Jean" is in no way
obliged to refer accurately to items of historical reality.

In a sense, the opening sentence already
"contains" the fictional destiny of Notre-Dame-
des-Fleurs, since the photographic image of Weidmann, truncated, implies a grisly end. In particular the phrase "un jour de septembre pareil
à celui où fut connu le nom de Notre-Dame-des-
Fleurs" mystifies and intrigues by the rapidity
with which it passes, precisely, from the known
into the unknown, the passage being effected by
the paradoxical "connu." The nouns "jour" and
"septembre" are referentials whose meaning is apparent; but Notre-Dame-des-Fleurs is an unknown
entity, an anaphoric whose significance will derive from repetition in the as yet unread text;
nonetheless, his presence in the "Weidmann"
sentence implies the probability of a similar
fate. In the same phrase the reader is again
plunged into the unknown by an ambiguous temporal
imprecision. Despite the specification of hour,
month and nation, oddly but improbably reminiscent of that debated beginning "la marquise sor-
tit à cinq heures," and despite Weidmann's look
of wounded airman, suggestive of the war, the
sentence is again led into abstraction by the
phrase "...pareil à celui où fut connu..." Thus
Genet prepares the transition from an immediate
(meaning conveyed by words alone) to a distant
(meaning conveyed in relation to the text) temporality.

Indeed, the opening pages of Notre-Dame-
des-Fleurs evince an extremely complex set of
temporal conventions. This complexity results
partly from its structural embedding, with the
duality that this imposes; and partly from the
fictional self-consciousness responsible for that
embedding. It might first seem that the novel's
dual structure would correspond conveniently to

the theoretical distinction between <u>Erzählte Zeit</u>
and <u>Erzählzeit</u> - or, in the words of Todorov,
"(la temporalité) de l'univers représenté et celle
du discours le représentant."⁵ Jean's declaration
of intent - the ambiguities and imprecisions of
the initial sentence notwithstanding - seems to
indicate that this self-conscious meditation in
the frame is largely simultaneous to the act of
composing it, leading to a sort of prediction of
the story to come:

> Personne ne peut dire si je
> sortirai d'ici, ni, si j'en sors,
> quand ce sera.
>
> A l'aide donc de mes amants
> inconnus, je vais écrire une his-
> toire. Mes héros ce sont eux, collés
> au mur, eux et moi qui suis là,
> bouclé. Au fur et à mesure que vous
> lirez, les personnages, et Divine
> aussi, et Culafroy, tomberont du
> mur sur mes pages comme feuilles
> mortes, pour fumer mon récit.
>
> Et (je veux) refaire à ma guise,
> et pour l'enchantement de ma cellule
> (je veux dire que grâce à elle ma
> cellule sera enchantée), l'histoire
> de Divine que je connus si peu,
> l'histoire de Notre-Dame-des-Fleurs,
> et, n'en doutez pas, ma propre
> histoire.
>
> (<u>O.C. II</u>, pp. 12-13)

Professed at this juncture, Jean's actual, though
minimal, acquaintance with Divine - "Divine que
je connus si peu" - suggests an impending shift
to a posterior narration (or narration after the
fact) and prepares a bridge between the primary
and secondary recitations. Subsequent references
to conversations with Divine will indeed suggest
that she has told portions of her tale to Jean
at some indeterminate moment in the prison. One
might hope that the temporal problems of <u>Erzählte
Zeit</u>, resulting from the inevitable distortions
of all fiction, would be most apparent in the
inner story of Divine. However, this is not
entirely the case.

The secondary narrative begins rather abruptly with a statement of Divine's decease, an event which determines the ensuing problematical chronology: "Divine est morte hier au milieu d'une flaque si rouge de son sang vomi..." (O.C. II, p. 13) Everything - that is, the secondary narrative, the act of writing it, that particular moment in Jean's meditation - is accordingly situated in a sort of absolute "today," so that the progress of the novel becomes a measure for the passing of fictional time itself. In addition to "narrated" and "narrating" time, therefore, one discerns a third degree of temporality which I shall call "temps de l'écriture" or "writing time." Two hundred pages later, at the story's end, Divine lies dying, dies in fact; "Morte Divine," asks the narrator, "Que me reste-t-il à faire" (O.C. II, p. 205). The narrated deeds of Divine therefore finish at a point which would logically situate them just before they start, leaving the narrator to ruminate, in utter termination, upon his own expectations of liberation - "Et si demain j'étais libre?" - and, contingent upon an adverse verdict, the reincarnation of his characters:

> Et si je suis condamné?...je referai, pour l'enchantement de ma cellule, à Mignon, Divine, Notre-Dame et Gabriel d'adorables vies nouvelles.
>
> (O.C. II, p. 206)

Concomitant with its double structure the novel is thus doubly cyclical, since the termination of the secondary narrative returns the reader to its temporal inception, while the termination of the framing meditation repeats the initial formula "pour l'enchantement de ma cellule" and anticipates the possibility of resurrection.

Despite this tidy symmetry, the secondary narrative does not, after some prodigious feat of necessary flashback, advance smoothly from the statement "Divine est morte hier..." to the comp-

lementary announcement "...Divine mourait" at
proceeding's close. There ensues an intricate
continuum of anachronies or disproportions in
narrated and narrating time, so that flashback
and digression, anticipation and omission, far
from reflecting an absence of structure, on the
contrary constitute the complex articulation of
the novel's jerky plot. The death of Divine
actually constitutes a false departure, since
the funeral sequence which follows hard upon it
renews the pretext for the novel: "Puisque
Divine est morte, le poète peut la chanter...
Je vous parlerai de Divine..." (O.C. II, p. 23).
The "Divine-Saga" then starts afresh with a
flashback of some twenty years to the time when
a slender, startling young Divine first embarks
on her career as a prostitute; her outrageous
garb repells all prospective clients but Mignon,
who is too drunk to notice. With the aid of
"Divinarianes," anecdotic miniatures of Divine's
personal oddities, the next twenty-five pages
re-create ten idyllic domestic years in the long
love-affair of Mignon and Divine, broken only by
a brief divorce in which Mignon leaves Divine
for her friend Mimosa II.

At this juncture, that is, in crudely
fractional terms, about one-quarter-way through
the book, there occurs an abrupt shift of narrative focus, heralding the advent and briefly
encompassing the crime of the titular assassin,
Mignon's illegitimate progeny. Coincidence determines the adolescent's subsequent destiny;
fleeing with his booty via the Gare Saint-Lazare,
Notre-Dame drops his wallet; it is picked up by
Mignon. Unconscious incest takes them in and
out of luxury hotels and finally, the money
spent, back to Divine's attic in the rue Caulain-
court. A triangular affair ensues. Divine is
now entering upon the phase of her humiliations,
relieved temporarily by the virile soldier Gabriel,
an "Archangel" who almost loves the aging queen
before being speedily disposed of in the war.

In the absence of Notre-Dame, who has

set off for Marseille with an "invented" character Marchetti, and of Mignon, who has practically
deserted her, Divine lives for a while with the
negro Seck Gorgui, a dark antithesis of Gabriel;
Notre-Dame returns to create a further triangle.
This central portion of the narrative reaches its
climax in the drama of Divine's jealousy, aroused
at a drag ball on the rue Lepic when Notre-Dame-
des-Fleurs, radiant in a blue silk turn-of-the-
century gown, entrances Seck Gorgui; from their
reciprocal affection, Divine is excluded. To
retrieve the situation, she surrenders Notre-
Dame to Mimosa II, an ironic re-enactment of the
earlier divorce that will indirectly cause the
adolescent's ruin. The remaining fourth of narrative encompasses the arrest for theft, humiliation and imprisonment of Mignon, the arrest and
trial of Notre-Dame-des-Fleurs, and the ultimate
degradations and terminal illness of Divine; the
Divine-Saga is thus returned to the point of its
commencement.

Despite the frequent interruptions of
the narrator, his apparently digressive sallies
into the childhood of Divine, and the occasional
reports on masturbation which punctuate the recitation, the disposition of the major sequences
does impart a certain balance. The pattern is
chiefly dictated by the passions of Divine, which
might be schematically represented as going from
pair to triangle to pair in the relatively happy
period before the death of Gabriel, and from pair
to triangle to pair and general calamity in the
period of downfall.

Character creation in Notre-Dame-des-
Fleurs - a matter obviously influential in
Divine's fictional destiny - reflects both temporal problems and the novel's structural duality,
since most of the protagonists of the secondary
narrative seem modelled on persons purportedly
encountered in the frame. Principally, Jean comments on his own connection with Divine: "...
c'est mon destin, vrai ou faux, que je mets sur
les épaules de Divine," (O.C. II, p. 46) Func-

tioning as the narrator's <u>alter ego</u>, Divine possesses his creative powers:

> ...pour plus de sûreté, elle inventa
> Marchetti. Elle eut vite fait de lui
> choisir un physique, car elle possédait
> dans son imagination de fille isolée,
> pour ses nuits, une réserve de cuisses,
> de bras, de torses...
> (<u>O.C. II</u>, p. 72)

Instantaneously "invented" by Divine, Marchetti thus enters into the secondary narrative and sets off for Marseille with Notre-Dame. Mignon himself, the narrator declares, is suggested by memories of Roger-le-Corse, while Notre-Dame is the literary offspring of Jean's erotic veneration for Pilorge:

> Quand je la connus à Fresnes,
> Divine m'en parla beaucoup (de
> Mignon), cherchant son souvenir, la
> trace de ses pas, partout dans la
> prison, mais je ne sus jamais son
> visage avec exactitude, et ce m'est
> une séduisante occasion de faire ici
> qu'il se confonde dans mon esprit
> avec le visage et la stature de
> Roger.
> (<u>O.C. II</u>, p. 28)

> Ainsi Notre-Dame naquit de mon amour
> pour Pilorge, avec au coeur et sur
> ses dents bleutées le sourire que la
> peur, exorbitant ses prunelles, ne
> lui arrachera pas.
> (<u>O.C. II</u>, p. 64)

A further such example is the negro Seck Gorgui:

> Gorgui, notre nègre, était vif et
> vigoureux. Un mouvement de ses reins
> faisait vibrer la chambre, comme
> Village, l'assassin noir, le faisait
> de sa cellule en prison. J'ai voulu
> retrouver dans celle-ci, où j'écris

68

> aujourd'hui, l'odeur de la charogne
> que le nègre au fier fumet répandait,
> et grâce à lui, je puis un peu mieux
> donner vie à Seck Gorgui.
> (O.C. II, p. 103)

Seck does not exactly emerge from the narrator's
acquaintance with Clément Village, but is related
to Village by certain exaggerated racial characteristics - inordinate virility, blackness, smell
- and by textual proximity. That the narrator
returns consciously to the absolute present of
his "writing time" - "où j'écris aujourd'hui" -
incidentally demolishes the fictional illusion
of the secondary narrative, while re-establishing
the convention of its genesis.

Structural duplicity, temporal complica-
tions - most prominently, cyclic analepses or
flashbacks, themselves suddenly annihilated by
return to the narrator's present - occur in the
major sequences by which the Divine-Saga despite
itself advances. The funeral of Divine exempli-
fies these formal intricacies. If Divine dies
in the "yesterday" of the narrator's time, she is
interred in his "today." Jean's recounting of
the obsequies begins, accordingly, in the temporal
convention of "today:"

> Trois heures après-midi. Il pleut
> derrière les barreaux depuis hier
> et il fait du vent. Je me laisse
> aller comme au fond d'un océan, au
> fond d'un quartier sombre, de maisons
> dures et opaques, mais assez légères,
> au regard intérieur du souvenir, car
> la matière du souvenir est poreuse.
> Le grenier que Divine a habité si
> longtemps est au sommet d'une de ces
> maisons...
> (O.C. II, p. 14)

From exterior contemplation the narrator's revery
moves inward, dissolving material obstacles with
cinematic ease; the telescopic focus on Divine's
abode resembles a cinematic shot with zooming lens.

Revery soon develops into past narration, the
concrete, outer frame of Jean's interning cell
finding an interior equivalent in the attic of
Divine, in which mourns Ernestine her mother.
The funeral sequence embraces descriptions of
the great screaming fairies of Montmartre, Divine's former friends; the arrival of Mignon,
come to pay his last, indifferent respects; and
the indelicate fantasies of the local curate,
who dreams of having his member handled by the
graveside group. Yet the core of the sequence
is not the actual burial, but a burlesque incident which took place when Divine was a child,
Culafroy. Seriously ill, drugged with barbitu-
ates, Culafroy has been presumed moribund; to
make his death more poignant, the extravagantly
sensitive Ernestine attempts to shoot her ailing
child, failing with ridiculous results. Embellished by Ernestine's nuptial fantasies, the
episode plunges back to a time when Culafroy was
not even born. Since the semi-comatose child himself is dreaming of his boyhood lover, the episode
prefigures a moment at the novel's end: one of
the dying Divine's last lucid reminiscences concerns Alberto's comforting corduroy trousers.
Moreover, beginning with Mignon mounting Divine's
quasi-celestial stair, ending with Mignon be-
holding Ernestine still drunk with tragedy, the
incident is resolved into an almost perfect cycle.

It is natural that the presence of Ernestine beside the coffin should suggest a link between Divine's adult life and her past, just as
Jean's acquaintance with Divine provides a bridge
for his imaginings. This should not, however,
imply that the deeds of tiny Culafroy take place
within another, third narrative surround. In a
sense, the book is about the writing of a novel;
in another sense, it is the story of how Louis
Culafroy became Divine-la-Cascadeuse, the "mater-
nal" lover of Notre-Dame-des-Fleurs. This latter
metamorphosis is not related chronologically; the
narrator dips into the childhood of Divine at ir-
regular intervals and depths, revealing with each

backward plunge something of the sensibility
which, inherited from Ernestine, marks the child
and the adult. The result is a vertical, rather
than a horizontal, picture of an individual's
consciousness at any given moment; vertical, cyclic and instantaneous, leaving the reader free to
reconstruct a chronological progression if he
chooses.

Not least among its properties, the
funeral sequence contains one of the many startling instances of absolute, deliberate coincidence
of primary and secondary narrative. Describing
the screaming queens who are arriving at Divine's
abode, the narrator comments: "Des tantes-filles
portaient des couronnes, de celles précisément que
je fabrique dans ma cellule..." (O.C. II, p. 15).
Similar glass beads, strung together by the narrator, re-appear in Divine's coronation parody, an
event which must considerably precede her funeral:

> Les petites perles roulent dans
> la sciure semée sur le plancher où
> elles sont semblables aux perles de
> verre que les colporteurs vendent...
> et celles-ci sont pareilles aux perles
> de verre que nous enfilons chaque jour
> dans des kilomètres de fil de laiton...
> (O.C. II, p. 118)

Crown, frame or wreath, recurrent structural motif,
the glass beads resume in circular form the cycles
of the inner narrative.

The narratorial interventions which accompany the diverse apparitions of the beads come
close to exemplifying what Gérard Genette has
termed métalepse narrative.[6] Classical examples
provided by Genette of this "narrative transgression" include a story told by Cortazar about a
man murdered by a character in a novel he is reading; and Tristram Shandy, "narrateur extradiégétique"
or exterior to the story he is telling, requiring
his father inside the diégèse or narrative to pro-
long his siesta. Such transgressions, in which a

narrator or hypothetical reader literally steps
from one narrative level to another, are considered by Genette as indicative of the importance of narration itself:

> D'une certaine façon, le pirandellisme
> de Six personnages en quête d'auteur
> ou de Ce soir on improvise, où les
> mêmes acteurs sont tour à tour héros
> et comédiens, n'est qu'une vaste
> expansion de la métalepse, comme tout
> ce qui en dérive dans le théâtre de
> Genet, par exemple, et comme les
> changements de niveau du récit robbe-
> grilletien: personnages échappés d'un
> tableau, d'un livre, d'une coupure de
> presse, d'une photographie, d'un rêve,
> d'un souvenir, d'un fantasme, etc.
> Tous ces jeux manifestent par l'inten-
> sité de leurs effets l'importance de
> la limite qu'ils s'ingénient à franchir
> au mépris de la vraisemblance, et qui
> est précisément la narration (ou la
> représentation) elle-même; frontière
> mouvante mais sacrée entre deux mondes:
> celui où l'on raconte, celui que l'on
> raconte.[7]

In the case of Notre-Dame-des-Fleurs, where metalepsis invariably accompanies reference to the
act of creation, it seems that this "transgression" is a function of the primary narrative or
frame, whose principal subject or theme is,
precisely, the imaginative processes which engender the secondary story of Divine.

(c) Song and Dance

If the litany of crimes set elegantly
forth on the initial page of Notre-Dame-des-Fleurs
serves to introduce the purpose of the book - "Et
c'est en l'honneur de leurs crimes que j'écris mon
livre" - it also re-establishes the idiom of song,

already manifest in the poems as the operative
artifice for pouring forth:

> Cette merveilleuse éclosion de
> belles et sombres fleurs, je ne l'ai
> apprise que par fragments: l'un
> m'était livré par un bout de journal,
> l'autre cité négligemment par mon
> avocat, un autre dit, presque chanté,
> par les détenus, - leur chant devenait
> fantastique et funèbre (un De Profundis),
> autant que les complaintes qu'ils
> chantent le soir, que la voix qui
> traverse les cellules et m'arrivent
> troublée, désespérée, altérée.
>
> (O.C. II, pp. 9-10)

Elicited as an imaginary accompaniment to the
narrator's testimony, figuratively applied to
both the newspaper item and the prisoner's lament,
the "chant" is immediately evoked as a thematic
constant of the "frame."

When Divine has been pronounced dead and
buried, the narrator draws from this event a justification for poetic and balletic idioms:

> ...Divine est morte, morte et enterrée
> ...est morte et enterrée...

> Puisque Divine est morte, le poète
> peut la chanter, conter sa légende, le
> dict de Divine. La Divine-Sage devrait
> être mimée, dansée, avec de subtiles
> indications. L'impossibilité de la
> mettre en ballet m'oblige à me servir
> de mots lourds d'idées précises, mais
> je tâcherai de les alléger d'expressions
> banales, vides, creuses, invisibles.
>
> (O.C. II, pp. 23-4)

The italicised refrain, appropriated from "Mal-
brough s'en va-t-en guerre," represents a common
species of parody - parody, in fact, in its most
literal form - and suggests that the ensuing
"Divine-Saga" will be chanted on a borrowed air.

Whether presumed hummed by Divine's friends or
imagined as permeating the text with an invisible
refrain, the two lines in either case constitute
a song. That the consciously creative "I" presents the book as a blend of song and dance
obliges the reader to conceive of it as an artistic object and to imagine a potential choreography.
A supplementary aesthetic distance is added to
that already imposed by the structural frame.
Complementing the artifice of song established in
the outer frame, the inner recitation is rich in
melodious idiom. Emissions from stolen radios,
for example, punctuate the connubial idyll of
Mignon and Divine. Although specific references
to classical music are rather rare in Genet, such
emissions permit one of the novel's two, possibly
three, mentions of Mozart:[11]

> Divine n'a pas pu supporter l'audi-
> tion, à la radio, de la Marche de la
> Zauberflüte (sic).
> (O.C. II, p. 162)

The speech of characters is frequently akin to
song, as when Divine launches into her inverted
"litanies" of camp frivolities, dazzling the
dumb male Mignon and ceasing only when exhausted;
or when the chorus of select transvestites twit-
ters into sarcasm: "Le choeur des amies: Pitiah,
pitiah pour la Divhaine!" (O.C. II, p. 113). At
once pagan and musically Christian, the notion
of the chorus would seem to be embodied in the
group of queens who, led by Mimosa II, assemble
at the great ritual moments in the legend of
Divine: funeral, parody of coronation, transvestite balls, trial of Notre-Dame. Genet seems in
fact to have given conscious thought to the classical functions of the chorus, which is mentioned
in one of the narrator's meditations:

> Le matin, qu'une porte s'ouvre, -
> toutes alors sont fermées, et c'est
> un mystère profond, autant que le
> mystère du nombre chez Mozart ou que
> l'utilité du choeur dans la tragédie-
> ...
> (O.C. II, p. 197)

Though not exactly musical, Divine's strident
laugh, exaggerated and refined, rings out with
stylised operatic merriment. In addition to
these vociferations, the protagonists do from
time to time burst into song, as when Gabriel's
virile performances prompt him to intone the
Marseillaise, or when Notre-Dame erupts into
Taraboumdié (sic) as he descends the rue Lepic
in regal drag.

Most significant of the inner narrative's
refrains is the Veni Creator Spiritus which, together with the motif of the violin, haunts Divine
throughout her earthly divagations. A Pentecostal
and a nuptial hymn, the Veni Creator is heard
three times within the text. On the first occasion,
a tipsy Divine, apprehended by two stalwart cops,
wreaks comic transformation on the passers-by:

> Elle chante le Veni Creator d'une
> voix aiguë. En tous les passants
> naissent de petits couples de mariés
> voilés de tulle blanc, qui s'agenouil-
> lent sur un prie-Dieu de tapisserie;
> les deux sergents de ville se
> revoient garçons d'honneur à la noce
> d'une cousine...
> (O.C. II, p. 47)

In a central analeptic digression, in which there
occurs a miraculous sacrilege committed in the
village church, the narrator suggests the effect
of this hymn on the nascent sensibility of the
child Culafroy:

> Des hymnes inattendues et inouies
> sonnaient, parmi elles la plus
> troublante, ce Veni Creator qu'on
> chante aux messes de mariage. Le
> charme du Veni Creator était celui
> des dragées et des boutons de fleur
> d'oranger en cire,... Il est
> important d'en parler, car il est
> celui qui ravit au plau haut des
> cieux l'enfant Culafroy. Et je ne
> puis dire pourquoi.
> (O.C. II, p. 100)

That the nuptial qualities of the hymn would seem
so to trouble the small boy foreshadows, by
humorous euphemism, Divine's less than chaste
vocation. That it returns at the moment of her
death implies that she has finally become the
bride of God, a destiny ironically supposed, in
lesser circumstances, by the group of chanting
friends: "...voilà la Divine mariée à Dieu."
(O.C. II, p. 113) Evocative of the Holy Ghost
which descends at Pentecost and inspires the
disciples to "speak with tongues," the Veni
Creator permeates the life of Divine as an inner,
celestial antithesis to that invocation rising
from the depths, the mournful De Profundis of
the exterior, "cellular" frame.

The subtle indications inferred as potential choreography for the Saga of Divine may be
seen as aids in the translation of motion into
song, or song into motion; more precisely, since
most characters are at some point described in
terms of gait, of song into ambulation:

> Passa l'Eternel sous forme de
> mac. Les babils se turent. Nu-
> tête et très élégant, simple et souri-
> ant, simple et souple, arrivait
> Mignon-les-Petits-Pieds. Souple,
> il avait dans son allure la magnifi-
> cence lourde du barbare qui foule
> avec ses bottes crottées des four-
> rures de prix.
> (O.C. II, p. 15)

> Notre-Dame souriait et chantait.
> Il chantait comme une harpe éolienne,
> une brise bleutée passant au travers
> les fils de son corps; il chantait
> son corps; il n'aimait pas. La police
> ne le soupçonnait pas. Il ne soupçon-
> nait pas la police. Telle était
> l'indifférence de cet enfant, qu'il
> n'achetait même pas les journaux: il
> allait sa mélodie.
> (O.C. II, p. 81)

A number of persons make entrances that require
ascension or descent; Divine's spiral stair, for
instance, tortuous and remote to the point of illusion, furnishes pretext for several balletic
exits and descents. The ceremonial entrance of
Notre-Dame-des-Fleurs is made on the sombre stair-
case of crime, figurative steps which, as Brigid
Brophy has remarked in a perceptive article, resemble a trompe-l'oeil in that they suddenly become the literal stairway of the unsuspecting Sieur
Ragon. Even the soldier Gabriel is first represented in a vertical advance:

> Divine croyait Mignon au cinéma,
> Notre-Dame, voleur à l'étalage, dans
> un grand magasin, mais...chaussures
> américaines, chapeau très simple,
> gourmette d'or au poignet, - tout du
> mac en somme, - Mignon vers le soir
> descendait l'escalier du grenier, et
> ...Vint l'inévitable soldat.
>
> ...Gabriel apparut. Je le vois aussi
> descendre une rue présque verticale,
> courant...
>
> (O.C. II, p. 18)

The phrases which depict the descent of Mignon
themselves recur - "Chaussures américaines, chapeau
très souple...etc." (O.C. II, p. 124) - when
Mignon goes off to encounter Notre-Dame in the
garden of the Tuileries. The occasional repetition of such phrases, combined with the ambulatory
emphasis, imparts a degree of periodicity to the
novel; one might almost say the work is measured
by the tread of radiant pimps and soldiers. At
times, a classic verbal exercise of balance, repetition and alliteration not only conveys the man-
nerisms of an individual saunter but also, with
judicious inclusion of particulars, creates the
rhythmic equation for a whole existence:

> Notre-Dame-des-Fleurs, encore et
> déjà vêtu de son léger, flottant,
> jeune, fou de minceur et pour tout
> dire fantômal costume de flanelle

grise, qu'il portait le jour de son
crime et portera le jour de sa mort,
y vint   afin de prendre un billet
pour le Havre.
                        (O.C. II, p. 65)

Such "indications," ostensibly pertaining to the
fictional content of the secondary narrative, reflect in their rhythmic insistance the balletic
intentions expressed in the "frame."

Actual dancing is accomplished in the
Divine-Saga in the course of the transvestite
ball, and in the young activities of Culafroy, a
self-instructed dancer and violinist who himself
constructs a discouragingly squeaky instrument.
The passage devoted to Culafroy's apprenticeship
to ballet comes close to a defence of cratylism
in its choreographic interpretation of Nijinsky's
name:

Par l'allure du mot Nijinsky (la
montée de l'N, la descente de la
boucle du j, le saut de la boucle du
k et la chute de l'y, forme graphique
d'un nom qui semble vouloir dessiner
l'élan, avec ses retombées et rebondis-
sements sur le plancher, du sauteur
qui ne sait sur quel pied se poser),
il devina la légèreté de l'artiste,
comme il saura un jour que Verlaine
ne peut être que le nom d'un poète
musicien.
                        (O.C. II, p. 94)

Reminiscent, a trifle consciously perhaps, of
Symbolist alliances of sense and sound, of synthe-
ses of several arts, the passage proceeds with
descriptions of points and pirouettes executed
amid items of Ernestine's laundry, thereby con-
tributing, in one of the narrator's cyclic digressions, to the "vertical" portrait of Divine.

Additional evocations of the Belle Epoque
are found in the book's most evident balletic

scene, the drag ball in Montmartre. Festivities
take place in Le Tavernacle, a small cabaret re-
served, on Thursday nights, for the dynasty of
queens "et leurs Messieurs." The atmosphere which
then pervades the cabaret prompts Jean to inter-
ject: "Ce serait l'endroit rêvé pour commettre
un meurtre," a fantasy which reminds one of the
pseudonym "Murder Cabaret" accorded, in its heyday,
the Lapin Agile.[8] On the crucial occasion in
question, Divine produces two silk gowns:

> Divine a retrouvé pour ce soir ses
> deux robes de soie, d'époque 1900,
> qu'elle conserve, souvenir d'anciennes
> mi-carêmes. L'une est noire, brodée de
> jais; elle la mettra et propose l'autre
> à Notre-Dame.
>
> ...Il se baissa, se tourna, se regarda
> dans la glace. La robe, qui est à
> tournure, fait bien saillir sa croupe
> évocatrice de violoncelles. Mettons
> une fleur de velours dans ses cheveux
> ébouriffés...
>
> ...Divine met sa robe de soie noire,
> par-dessus, une jacquette rose, et prit
> un éventail de tulle pailletée.
> (O.C. II, p. 138)

A typical dress of that era left the shoulders
bare, had a narrow, plunging waist and usually a
bustle; its sleeves were ruched at the shoulder
or else narrow to the elbow, then flared and
scollopped at the cuff; the skirt descended in
flounces and ended in a brief train. Peculiarly
uncomfortable underwear was worn beneath, impart-
ing, to its wearer, the outline of an egg-timer.[9]
The flat-chested Notre-Dame, "nu sous la soie,"
is spared the petticoat and stays but not the
bustle; the portrayal of his rump - "sa croups
évocatrice de violoncelles" - being a pederastic
equivalent of the sandclock shape. The front of
his dress, however, is apparently tight enough to
reveal the embarrassing tumescence which causes
Seck to be gallant and Divine to be jealous. As
for the actual party, its swirl of silk and smoke

recall the jollity of Chéret's <u>Carnaval</u> or Lautrec's
<u>Moulin Rouge</u>:·

> Ils entrent dans un feu d'artifice
> éclaté en volants de soie et mousse-
> lines qui ne peuvent pas se dégager
> de la fumée. On danse la fumée. On
> fume la musique. On boit d'un bouche
> à l'autre. Les copains acclament...
> (<u>O.C. II</u>, pp. 138-9)

More of a realist than Chéret, Lautrec, it has
been said, did not "see the life of the demi-
monde through rose-coloured spectacles," but
combined a sense of the frivolous with an ability
to confront stark and sometimes sordid facts.[10]
This observation may be deemed pertinent to Genet's
description of Notre-Dame intoning <u>Tararaboumdié</u>
in silken travesty at the bottom of the rue Lepic:

> Au fait, il ressemblait à Emilienne
> d'Alençon. La tournure de cette
> robe bleue (ce qu'on appelait un
> faux-cul) attendrissait, jusqu'à le
> faire baver légèrement, le grand nègre
> glorieux. Divine les regardait dévaler
> vers la plage. Notre-Dame chantait
> parmi les poubelles. Pensez à quelque
> Eugénie Buffet blonde, en robe de soie,
> chantant un matin dans les cours, au
> bras d'un nègre en habit.
> (<u>O.C. II</u>, p. 141)

Eugénie Buffet the <u>diseuse</u> and Mme d'Alençon the
<u>cocotte</u> belong, supremely, to the Paris of the
late 1890's, Mme Buffet being depicted by Métivet
in posters, Mme d'Alençon being discussed in every
gossip column. The occurrence of these names,
together with the specific references to costume,
would seem to indicate that Genet was writing a
sort of pastiche of the <u>belle époque</u>, enlivened by
the spontaneity of poster art.

(d) The Part of Parody

Parodical elements enter <u>Notre-Dame-des-Fleurs</u> in ways both secular and Biblical. An example of the secular - a species of social parody - appears in Divine's mimesis, at once courageous and humiliating, of a royal coronation. The incident occurs in one of the bars frequented by Divine's friends, the dynasty of queens; Divine has been wearing a small tiara of glass beads which has fallen to the floor and smashed. To preserve face, she substitutes her dental bridge:

> Dans le cabaret, toutes les tantes
> sont soudain agenouillées. Seuls, les
> hommes s'érigent droits. Alors, Divine
> pousse un rire en cascade stridente.
> Tout le monde est attentif: c'est son
> signal. De sa bouche ouverte, elle
> arrache son dentier, le pose sur son
> crâne et, le coeur dans la gorge mais
> victorieuse, elle s'écrie d'une voix
> changée, et les lèvres dans la bouche:

> -Eh bien merde, mesdames, je
> serai reine quand même.
> (O.C.II, pp. 118-9)

This anecdote, which serves to illustrate the narrator's dictum that in his world laughter is always the result of painful drama, is peculiarly Genettian in its structural qualities: it is a double parody. The initial parody is the wearing of the tiara; this act is then duplicated by the auto-coronation, which in turn becomes self-parody. Transvestism, itself an aping of the strictly defined sexual polarities of straight society, further complicates the incident. Again, the tiara of glass beads recalls the wreaths and fake pearls which tend to accompany the narrative metalepses. Beyond these confusions, however, the incident serves to illustrate Genet's own sense of the incongruous. I insist on the singularity thereof, since critics generally aver that Genet is not comic; and indeed, not all readers are of necessity amused by the frivolities of transvestism,

particularly when these extend into religion.
Allowing that the major narrative sequences develop from Divine's amorous relationships,
the most significant are obviously her triangular
affairs with Mignon and Notre-Dame, Notre-Dame and
Gorgui. For the present purpose, these threesomes
may be termed Eternal Triangles - representations
both solemn and burlesque of the Holy Trinity itself. In the first such arrangement Mignon, the
archetypal pimp, appears as God: "Passa l'Eternel
sous forme de mac." (O.C. II, p. 15) Divine herself, precious as a sacred bird, is compared on
several occasions to the Holy Ghost:

> Pour lors, ils boivent du thé et
> Divine sait bien qu'elle l'avale comme
> un pigeon l'eau claire. Comme le
> boirait, s'il buvait, le Saint-
> Esprit en forme de colombe.
> (O.C. II, p. 34)

Divine exerts the powers of that spirit with un-
fortunate consequences for her friends. She has
the power of creation, exercised in her invention
of Marchetti, and radiates an intangible, treacherous influence that acts absurdly and fatally on
male minds. When, for example, the police arrest
Notre-Dame for smuggling opium, they are confronted
by a naked and dismembered tailor's model, a
startling sight which at once evokes ideas of
crime. The narrator imputes it to Divine: "Le
mannequin. Il faut reconnaître ici peut-être
l'influence de Divine. Elle est partout où sur-
git l'inexplicable." (O.C. II, p. 173) The inevitable associations conjured up by the model in
a sense necessitate Notre-Dame's confession of his
real crime, hence his decapitation. Divine's
theme song, the Veni Creator (Spiritus), itself
invokes the Holy Ghost; this invocation is turned
to parodical account when an inebriated Divine
sings it in the street, arrested by two stalwart
cops. Last but not least, her divinity is explicable in terms of her skilful performances in bed,
the most impressive of which have been excised

82

from Gallimard's commercial version of the text.

The attic in which Mignon and Divine
live out their connubial idyll resembles paradise;
a semi-celestial abode, situated in the highest
part of Paris, and attended by cohorts of invisible angels:

> Ainsi le couple vit sans cahots.
> Le concierge, du bas de l'escalier,
> veille sur leur bonheur. Et vers le
> soir, les anges balayent la chambre,
> font le ménage. Pour Divine, les
> anges sont des gestes qui se font sans
> elle.
>
> (O.C. II, p. 36)

Into this idyllic household and to complete the
Trinity drifts Notre-Dame-des-Fleurs, whom Mignon
has begotten sixteen years previously. The question of paternity is resolved in a passage which
Gallimard, perhaps suspecting blasphemy, again
excised from the original edition:

> Mignon l'avait fait un matin
> d'avril (ce qui le fit naître en
> décembre) à une fruitière de la
> rue Lepic, dont nous ne saurons
> jamais rien. Seize ans plus tard,
> le père et le fils devaient se
> retrouver juste à temps pour dévorer ensemble les vingt mille francs
> du vieux étranglé.[11]

Although Divine cannot actually give birth, her
symbolic impregnation is implied in a manner that
recalls both the immaculate conception and pagan
myth:

> Mignon aime Divine de plus en
> plus profondément... Mais de plus
> en plus la néglige. Elle reste
> seule au grenier, elle offre à Dieu
> son amour et sa peine. Car Dieu -
> les Jésuites l'ont dit - choisit
> mille manières d'entrer dans les
> âmes: la poudre d'or, un cygne, un

taureau, une colombe, qui sait comment encore? Pour un gigolo qui fait
les tasses, peut-être choisit-il une
méthode que la théologie n'a pas
cataloguée, peut-être choisit-il
d'être Tasse. On peut aussi se de-
mander quelle forme, les Eglises
n'existant pas, eût pris la sainteté
(je ne dis pas la voie de son salut)
de Divine et de tous les saints.
(O.C. II, pp. 58-9)

Much later, in the trial of Notre-Dame, Divine
will testify of the assassin, "Il pourrait être
mon fils." (O.C. II, p. 188) Her functions therefore impinge upon those of the Virgin Mary.
Rather than leading to her glorification, however, the immaculate conception signals the start
of Divine's humiliations: far from being the
most favoured among women, she will be the most
reviled. Anticipating her misfortunes, the narrator announces that they will be temporarily
offset by the advent of the soldier Gabriel.
Although Gabriel does not actually appear for
another twenty-five pages, his name is placed,
significantly, in the very sentence that precedes
the criminal advent of Notre-Dame-des-Fleurs,
thus tracing a faint parallel with the Annuncia-
tion.

        In the second Trinity the negro Seck,
himself a dark antithesis of the blond "Archangel"
Gabriel, replaces an absent Mignon and becomes
the virile lover of Notre-Dame-des-Fleurs.
Throughout the novel Notre-Dame is cast both as
Christ and His mother. This parodical confusion
of identities, complicated by incest in the Trinities, seems a logical if irreverent outcome of
Christianity's more tangled doctrines concerning
the multiplicity of Christ. The young assassin's
pseudonym - Notre-Dame-des-Fleurs - suggests some
poetical cult of the Virgin, the comic possibilities of which are exploited after his arrest:

        Du jour au lendemain, le nom de

> Notre-Dame-des-Fleurs fut connu de
> la France entière, et la France est
> habituée aux confusions...Le curé
> d'un village, entendant autour de
> lui flotter le nom de Notre-Dame-des-
> Fleurs, sans en avoir reçu de mande-
> ment du diocèse, un dimanche en
> chaire, ordonna des prières et
> recommanda ce nouveau culte à la
> dévotion particulière des fidèles.
> Les fidèles, dans leurs banc, saisis,
> ne dirent pas un mot, ne pensèrent
> pas une pensée.
> (O.C. II, pp. 175-6)

At his trial, to the great shock of certain critics,
Notre-Dame is presented as the Immaculate Conception. His paradoxical innocence, the product, one
suspects, of his unadulterated stupidity, is indicated early in the book: "Il était - on peut dire
- l'assassin innocent." (O.C. II, p. 64) His
photograph, swallowed by Mimosa II in a parody of
the Holy Eucharist, becomes the Host: "Je l'adore,
ta Notre-Dame, je la communie." (O.C. II, p. 127)
The terse sentences which describe his execution
contain allusions to the Redeemer, and later, to
the death of Christ:

> Notre-Dame-des-Fleurs eut la tête
> coupée par un vrai couteau. Et rien
> ne se passa. A quoi bon? Il ne faut
> pas que le voile du temple se déchire
> de bas en haut parce qu'un dieu rend
> l'âme. Cela ne peut que prouver la
> mauvaise qualité de l'étoffe et sa
> vétusté: Quoique l'indifférence fût
> de rigueur, j'accepterai encore qu'un
> garnement irrévérencieux le troue d'un
> coup de pied et se sauve en criant au
> miracle. C'est clinquant et très bon
> pour servir d'armature à la Légende.
> (O.C. II, pp. 194-5)

If Genet's habit of ceremoniously inflating the
incongruous constitutes one comic procedure, the

flat, anti-climactic tone of this "miraculous"
conclusion implements an ironic reduction. It
also underlines the hero's dual role as god and
man. If Mignon, his father, is both God and
quintessential Man - "l'homme pareil à celui que
Michel-Ange peignit nu dans le Jugement dernier"
(O.C. II, p. 35) - Notre-Dame will logically become the son of man, a figure subject to his
author's simultaneous use of banality and pomp.

Incestuous Trinities and parodical duplicity are thus intrinsic to the overall structure of Notre-Dame-des-Fleurs. If the triangular
affair between Mignon, Divine and Notre-Dame dominates the first half of the book, that between
Notre-Dame, Divine and Seck Gorgui similarly
shapes its second half. Since the Trinities are
explicitly human, implicitly and comically celestial, human imperfection enters with Divine's
jealousy. When the presence of Notre-Dame proves
incommodious to Divine in the earlier relationship,
she sends him to Marseille with Marchetti; later,
rendered desperately jealous by the love of Notre-
Dame and Seck, she disposes of the young assassin
by means of Mimosa II. Jealousy is therefore a
further cause of Notre-Dame's arrest; once despatched from the attic, he no longer benefits
from Divine's protection but continues to suffer
the nefarious effects of her "poetic" influence.
The outcome of the inner narrative - Notre-Dame's
death at the guillotine - is in this way determined by the two triangular affairs.

It is perhaps prudent to point out in
conclusion that literary works involving allegory,
symbolic parallels or parody rarely fit the original pattern with exactitude, and Genet's novel is
certainly no facsimile of the New Testament.
Comic effect, however, may be said to reside in
this degree of distortion. The Biblical nature of
the parody implicates the major characters in
duality inasmuch as they are gods and men. Once
again, duality affects the existence of those characters in that their creation bears witness to
the novel's frame.

The dual structure of <u>Notre-Dame-des-Fleurs</u>, together with the autogenesis contained within that structure naturally emphasise the theme of creativity. This, incidentally, is an additional effect of parody - comic differences between the implicit and the actual models tend to draw attention to the latter, to the explicit work which parodies and the way in which it does so. This pre-occupation with literary creativity is typical of all Genet's works, but particularly of his early poems - <u>Le Condamné à mort</u> and <u>Marche funèbre</u> - and his first three novels, in which autocriticism and autogenesis accompany the establishment of frames.

NOTES TO CHAPTER II

[1]Violette Leduc provides the following account
of the publication of Notre-Dame:

-Genet était en prison, commença Cocteau,
je me demandais qui, dans Paris, lirait
le premier son manuscrit de Notre-Dame-des-
Fleurs. Je le portai chez Valéry. "Re-
viens dans huit jours, je te dirai ce que
j'en pense," me dit Paul Valéry.
-Alors?
-Attends. J'y retourne huit jours
après...
-Alors? Alors?
-Devine ce qu'il m'a dit.
-Que c'était génial!
-Il m'a dit: "Jean, il faut brûler ça.
Ça nous dérangerait." J'ai repris le manu-
scrit, je m'en suis occupé.
-Je ne peux pas le croire.
-C'est pourtant vrai, a dit Cocteau.

From La Folie en tête (Paris: Gallimard, 1970),
pp. 226-7.

[2]Lionel Abel, review of Our Lady of the Flowers in
New York Review of Books, I, no 4(Oct. 17, 1963),
p. 7.

[3]Oeuvres Complètes, II, p. 9. All subsequent
references to this edition will be bracketed into
the text, e.g. (O.C. II, p. 16).

[4]One of the editorial board of Degré Second -
probably Philip Thody - accepting an article by
the present author.

[5]Tzvetan Todorov, Poétique (Paris: Seuil, 1968),
p. 52.

[6]Gérard Genette, Figures III (Paris: Seuil, 1972),
pp. 243-5.

88

[7]Genette, _Figures III_, p. 245.

[8]"...these quarrels came to a head at a bar...in
the _Lapin Agile_ (Agile Rabbit), popularly known
as the murder cabaret, which was frequented by
the _durs_, the tough lads of the district..."
Hermann Schardt, _Paris 1900: Masterworks of
French Poster Art_ (New York: G.P. Putnam's
Sons, 1970), p. 11.

[9]"Nichts Unnatürlicheres als diese zwei Kurven -
in der Seitenansicht ein S-Zeichen mit der Taille
als Schwingangel -, die der Frau die Silhouette
eine Sanduhr gaben." Maurice Rheims, _Kunst um
1900_ (Vienna: Anton Schroll, 1965), p. 361.

[10]See Hermann Schardt, p. 20.

[11]Genet, _Notre-Dame-des-Fleurs_ (Monte Carlo, "aux
dépens d'un amateur," septembre, 1944), p. 82.
Catalogued as B.N. Enfer 1401.

CHAPTER III: <u>MIRACLE DE LA ROSE</u>

(a) Genesis and Time

Miracle de la Rose, Genet's second novel,
is dated "La Santé. Prison des Tourelles, 1943,"
and, like its predecessor, would appear to have
been composed in jail; the text bears ample witness
to incarceration, including claims that the un-
finished manuscript was concealed in a prison toilet
bowl. Like Notre-Dame-des-Fleurs, Miracle encompasses three periods of time: the narrator's childhood, passed in the reform school of Mettray in
Touraine; his manhood, a part of which is passed in
the daunting Central prison of Fontevrault, and a
sort of literary present, in which the book self-
consciously develops. Genet thus repeats, with
certain perceptible modifications - most notably,
the absence of a secondary narrator - the major
structural devices employed in Notre-Dame-des-
Fleurs. The episodes of past narrated time concern
the narrating "Jean Genet's" amorous escapades,
while the absolute present reflects the literary
perspective he imposes on them.

The immediacy which characterises the
opening sentences of Notre-Dame is stamped upon
the start of Miracle. "De toutes les Centrales
de France," begins the narrator, "Fontevrault est
la plus troublante." He thus establishes with
promptitude the scene of action: prison. Summa-
rised in this initial paragraph are the novel's
quintessential themes, which derive from darkly
potent connotations of the name of Fontevrault: its
royal and monastic past, its connections with the
Reformatory of Mettray, its troubling prestige
acquired through the presence, in the death cell, of
Harcamone the double murderer. There follows an
introductory segment of some seven pages in which
the narrator recalls his cold, uncomfortable jour-
ney to Fontevrault from Paris, commenting of the
train which conveyed him: "C'est là, en entrant
dans la voiture cellulaire, que je me sentis deve-
nir un visionnaire exact, désenchanté." (O.C. II,
p. 225) This pronouncement echoes the formula
"...pour l'enchantement de ma cellule" of Notre-
Dame-des-Fleurs. Having described his arrival, the

narrator comes to state his literary aim:

> Je vais tenter d'écrire ce que me
> fut Harcamone et, à travers lui, ce
> que me furent Divers, et Bulkaen sur-
> tout que j'aime encore et qui m'indique
> finalement mon destin... Par Harcamone,
> Divers et Bulkaen, je vais encore revivre
> Mettray qui fut mon enfance. Je vais
> retrouver la colonie pénitentiaire
> abolie, le bagne d'enfants détruit.
> (O.C. II, p. 230)

The novelist-narrator thus presents himself as
directly involved with his characters, themselves
instrumental in his quest for the childhood world
of Mettray, miraculous and lost. As in Notre-Dame-
des-Fleurs a self-conscious narrator presents movements of his mind which appear simultaneous to his
récit, and announces the impending book. Unlike
Notre-Dame, however, the récit to come paradoxically involves a return to the narrator's own
past. His perspective may thus be deemed at once
anticipatory and retrospective. The peculiar tension which results from this initial paradox is a
property of the novel's frame, in this case a
temporal one.

Like "Jean Genet," Harcamone, Divers and
Bulkaen are all "graduates" of Mettray, fitted by
that rigorous education for the formidable cells
of Fontevrault. Their relationships with the narrator determine the structure of the novel. Harcamone,
whom Jean knew slightly at Mettray, represents the
ultimate degree of criminality to which a pupil
of that institution can attain. Resuscitating an
old tradition of Mettray - "Tous les marles de
Mettray furent la fiancée mystique de quelque dur"
- Jean engages in a cult of Harcamone, becoming in
effect his mystical betrothed. This privileged
estate enables him to make great spiritual exer-
tions on behalf of the condemned man. Since all
the other prisoners hold Harcamone in similar
esteem, his largely invisible presence dominates
both the prison and the book. He appears, directly,

only once or twice; his most startling apparition
is a prefiguration of his death. Jean has been at
Fontevrault one week, and is being shaved with
some other convicts in the courtyard, when a mana-
cled Harcamone is brought out for exercise. Ecsta-
tic with recognition, Jean is inspired to an imaginative transformation and symbolic act: his idol's
handcuffs are suddenly transmuted into chains of
white roses. Taking the barber's scissors, Jean
cuts a white rose hanging near the condemned man's
wrist; the decapitated flower falls among the
locks of dirty hair, causing Harcamone almost to
faint. At the time of his execution by guillotine,
Harcamone is transfigured, in Jean's most testing
spiritual exercise, into the Mystical Rose. His
death - the "Miracle of the Rose" anticipated in
the title, the shaving scene, and diverse allusions
to roses - concludes the work, leaving the narrator
to meditate, in termination:

> Harcamone est mort, Bulkaen est
> mort. Si je sors, comme après la
> mort de Pilorge, j'irai fouiller les
> vieux journaux. Comme de Pilorge,
> il ne me restera plus entre les mains
> qu'un article très court, sur un
> mauvais papier... Ces papiers sont
> leur tombeau. Mais je transmettrai
> très loin dans le temps leur nom...
> leur nom troublera comme la lumière
> nous trouble qui arrive d'une étoile
> morte il y a mille ans. Ai-je dit
> tout ce qu'il fallait dire de cette
> aventure? Si je quitte ce livre, je
> quitte ce qui peut se raconter. Le
> reste est indicible.
> (O.C. II, p. 469)

The disposition of deaths thus resembles that of
Notre-Dame-des-Fleurs, in which the narrative begins and ends with death scenes of Divine. Mention
of Pilorge in this concluding paragraph recalls
the literary aims of both the first novel and Le
Condamné à mort; to the motif of the quest it adds,
in Miracle de la Rose, the desire to perpetuate

the memory of executed friends.

Amorous attachment binds the narrator
to both Divers and Bulkaen. Like Harcamone, Divers
is of Jean's generation; he was formerly Jean's
"husband" in an unconsummated marriage parodically
enacted at Mettray. The much younger Bulkaen, whom
Jean meets at Fontevrault and instantly adores,
represents the missing years, the link between the
worlds of the child and the adult. The narrative
which unfolds between the two depictions of Harcamone's decapitation contains episodes, not
chronologically disposed, pertaining to both
worlds. Despite the multiplicity of flashbacks
and digressions, the story is quite simple: Bulkaen, who does not love Jean, takes advantage of
the latter's passion by accepting gifts of bread
and tobacco, which he promptly passes on to his
own boyfriend Rocky. Much of the narrative's psychological interest is centered upon Jean's anxious
erotic speculations; who, he wonders, are Bulkaen's
other suitors? Will Bulkaen return his love? Despite an ejaculation accomplished by Jean in the
course of an odd, erotic battle, union with Bulkaen
is never properly achieved, for the boy is shot by
guards while attempting to escape. Meanwhile, however, Jean has acceded to the punitory Salle de
Discipline, where he beholds Divers seated on the
public lavatory; the humiliating aspects of this
meeting do not destory their long-frustrated affection. Two weeks after Bulkaen's death, and at the
time of Harcamone's decapitation, the narrator comments of this long-awaited consummation:

> Nous accomplissions quelque chose
> comme les noces d'or des époux
> douloureux et qui ne s'aiment plus
> dans la joie, mais dans la douleur.
> Nous avions attendu quinze ans, en
> nous cherchant peut-être sur d'autres
> mecs, depuis l'instant de mon départ
> de Mettray, alors que lui-même était
> au quartier pour quelque délit de
> gosse.
> (O.C. II, p. 468)

With these dolorous nuptials the two worlds are
joined; with Bulkaen dead, Harcamone beheaded,
and Divers successfully sodomised, destiny is
satisfied and the novel comes full circle.

Despite certain temporal and thematic
similarities with Notre-Dame-des-Fleurs, the structural properties of the two early novels are not
precisely similar. For one thing, Miracle is less
readily analysed in terms of structural divisions -
quarters, halves, and so on; for another, the pro-
tracted cyclic digressions of Notre-Dame-des-Fleurs
have largely disappeared. If a narrative pattern
can be established in Miracle, it is one of oscil-
lation between the two worlds - Mettray and Fontevrault - present in the narrator's mind. Since
Jean is actively engaged in most of the events depicted, his intervening ruminations do not at first
seem much distinguished from the body of the text.
The result is a certain attenuation of the frame,
whose existence critics have either implicitly con-
tested or ignored. In Notre-Dame-des-Fleurs, the
narratorial consciousness of literary creation is
a feature both of structure and of theme. For Dante
Ughetti this consciousness, as manifest in Miracle,
is a matter of theme alone:

> Nel Miracle de la Rose ... sono
> evidenti fra l'altre due temi, che
> ci sembrano fondamentali del mondo
> poetico creato da questo scrittore:
> la presa di coscienza, da parte dell'
> Autore, del suo destino, e la meditazione
> sull'attiva artistica, sulla sua autonomia,
> sul particolare modo per cui se presenta
> come forma singolare di conoscenza.[1]

The two themes - awareness of destiny, and consciousness of art - are in reality one, according to
Ughetti, since the form of the novel in effect coincides with the realisation of Genet's individual
destiny.

The extent to which "la meditazione sull'
attiva artistica" does result in structural duality

appears from rapid analysis of the novel's temporal
axes. In Notre-Dame-des-Fleurs the level of time
which most imposes itself upon chronological consideration of the "story" is the span encompassing
the Parisian, adult life of Divine and her acquaintance with Notre-Dame. Similarly, it is the "adult"
events at Fontevrault, culminating in the titular
"miracle," which suggest the most evident chronology. The number of days passed by Harcamone in the
death cell tallies almost exactly with the days
noted by Jean as pertinent to his affection for
Bulkaen. Harcamone is in that cell about forty-
seven days, in all: forty-five for the "pourvoi en
cassation," perhaps two more before his execution.
He has been there ten days when Jean arrives:
"Quand j'arrivai à la Centrale de Fontevrault,
depuis dix jours Harcamone était aux fers." (O.C.
II, p. 252) Jean has been in prison for about a
week - "Je vécus huit jours dans l'imprécision de
l'arrivée" (O.C. II, p. 232) - before he cuts the
rose; next day, he meets Bulkaen: "Le lendemain...
je devais l'oublier, pris par Bulkaen...J'étais à
Fontevrault depuis une semaine." (O.C. II, p. 235)
The friendship between Jean and Bulkaen, documen-
ted by such comments as "c'était le onzième jour
de notre rencontre," lasts about fifteen days,
until the latter's death. When Harcamone is executed, Bulkaen has been dead for at least eleven
days, plus four nights Jean spends in vigil: "il
y avait quatre jours que je travaillais mes nuits
...Il y avait quinze jours que Bulkaen était mort;"
(O.C. II, p. 450) "Il avait été exécuté onze jours
après que Bulkaen eut été fusillé." (O.C. II,
p. 465) All this adds up to forty-seven; ten days,
then one week, then two weeks, then two more. The
point of this pedantic demonstration is that the
chronology of the Fontevrault narrative is fairly
consistent, arithmetically almost exact; such imprecisions as it seems to contain enhance the
verisimilitude of Jean's supposed memory, since
exact retrospection of a period of forty-seven
days would seem rather hard.

The chronology of Jean's meditation or

"writing time," however, presents certain difficulties. Jean claims to be writing from the
"cellule de punition," while Harcamone is still
alive:

> Tous les jours, il allait à
> la promenade une heure, dans un
> préau spécial. Le préau n'était
> pas très loin de la cellule de
> punition où j'écris. Et ce que
> j'ai pris très souvent pour le
> bruit de ma plume contre l'encrier,
> c'était, derrière le mur, le
> bruit... des chaines du condamné
> à mort.
>
> (O.C. II, p. 257)

"Tous les jours, il allait" constitutes a summary
of an habitual action, an iterative condensation
which obviously occupies less narrating time than
it does represented or narrated time; the "était,"
"j'ai pris" and "c'était" of the next two sentences
clearly refer to the same period of narrating time,
implying that Jean wrote while Harcamone took his
walk; the present "j'écris," however, must designate the absolute writing time of an implied "today."
Once again, this implicit "today" is not to be confused with narrating time, which cannot designate
itself; the "temps de l'écriture" is thus inevitably fictional.

Towards the novel's end, Jean speaks of
his literary endeavours with similar temporal complexity:

> Je sortais chaque matin pour
> aller à la salle de discipline et
> ma cellule restait vide, nue. Je
> ne gardais, en les dissimulant dans
> la tinette, que les sacs en papier
> sur lequel je notai ce qui va suivre.
>
> (O.C. II, p. 450)

This observation is situated just before the narration of Harcamone's demise and the Miracle of the
Rose. Again, an iterative condensation or summary

designates a block of time presumably consequent
to that of Harcamone's walks; but the phrase "sur
lequel je notai ce qui va suivre" suggests either
that the narrator is recounting Harcamone's last
four nights for the second time, or that Jean is
at a temporal remove from the Jean who "noted"
what is to follow; in either case, there is duplicity, since the narrator refers to an anterior
act of writing. An ultimate temporal gap between
Genet and his narrator becomes apparent when, at
the book's close, one reads the purported date and
place of composition: "La Santé. Prison des
Tourelles, 1943." Genet does not date the work
to Fontevrault at all, and the absolute present
suggested by such observations as "Sur le mur de
ma cellule de punition, je viens de lire des
graffiti amoureux," must be considered fictional,
and proper to the novel's tenuous meditative
frame. At the beginning of the novel, the narrator claims to have left La Santé for Fontevrault
in the winter of the summer when Paris was first
occupied - 1940. The date "1943" is thus itself
a part of fiction, or else refers to a succeeding
incarceration.

        The difficulties which beset discussion
of the temporal frames of Miracle de la Rose derive therefore from apparent oscillations in the
narratorial temporal perspective. Gérard Genette
has posited four such temporal positions; posterior,
anterior, simultaneous and intercalated.[2] Miracle
seems to benefit from several, if not all, of these
conventions. Jean's view of the events described
at Mettray, and of the forty-seven days at Fontevrault, is clearly posterior; on the other hand, the
present tenses of the "cellule de punition" seem
fleetingly simultaneous. Inasmuch as the composition of the book is a narrated act, moments of the
récit seem, briefly, anterior or predictive - "ce
qui va suivre" - or even intercalated. The confusion which the reader possibly may feel, confronted by the "narrated act" of writing, is no
doubt due to yet another clause of temporal logic
postulated by Genette: "l'on sait que même les
récits d'anticipation...postdatent presque tou-

jours leur instance narrative, implicitement postérieure à leur histoire - ce qui illustre bien
l'autonomie de cette instance par rapport au moment de l'écriture réelle."[3]

(b) Internal Duplication and Mise en Abyme

      Among the diverse images, symbols and
themes characteristic of most texts by Genet, three
motifs from Miracle de la Rose impose themselves
upon a structural consideration of the book: circles, literary messages within the texts, and
flowers. In so far as the end of the narrative
marks the end of the literary quest - "je vais
tenter d'écrire ce que me fut Harcamone et, à
travers lui, ce que me furent Divers, et Bulkaen
surtout..." - a cycle of destiny is accomplished
by virtue of the novel. In one sense, temporal
and structural peculiarities emphasise the primacy
of creativity; in another, numerous references to
literature and song reinforce that emphasis thematically.

      The power of the written word is sugges-
ted in a little sequence in the opening seven pages.
The narrator reports how, arriving at Fontevrault,
he was obliged, ridiculously, to make the military
salute:

> Je croisai deux auxiliaires
> suivis d'un jeune garde et d'un
> greffier qui portaient sur en bran-
> card les huit livres monumentaux
> sur lesquels sont inscrits les noms
> des mille cent cinquante détenus...
> Je faillis saluer, non les géoliers,
> mais les livres qui contenaient le
> trop illustre nom d'Harcamone.
> (O.C. II, p. 228)

Obviously "monumental" in size, the books also entomb and preserve the names of the convicts, just
as the prison preserves its inmates whose faces,
Jean elsewhere declares, remain astonishingly

young. Two pages later, Jean heralds his own impending book, itself a memorial to Harcamone and Bulkaen.

Other "texts" contained within the major text are the poems Jean composes in honour of Harcamone and Divers, and the series of letters exchanged by the narrator and Bulkaen. This epistolary interchange, necessitated by the physical difficulties of communicating freely in a prison, influences the progress of the relationship which itself subsequently constitutes a portion of the book. Furthermore, the one letter of Bulkaen to be reproduced almost in entirety indicates the narrator's syntactic superiority and awareness of same:

> Mon petit Jeannot,
>
> Merci de ton mot qui m'a fait
> plaisir, mais excuse-moi si, de
> mon côté, je ne peux te faire des
> lettres dans le genre de la tienne,
> il me manque l'instruction pour
> cela car ce n'est pas à Mettray que
> j'ai pu apprendre avec le père
> Guépin...
>
> (O.C. II, pp. 276-7)

One learns in the next paragraph that Bulkaen has bidden adieu to his former lover Rocky who is being deported to the penal colony. The poem, if written, would constitute a structural anticipation, or mise en abyme, of what Jean considers Bulkaen's destiny ought to have been. Jean adds that it is Bulkaen whom he evoked in the "bagne" of Le Condamné à mort, a remark which tempts one to biographical supposition. If the events described at Fontevrault are dated Christmas 1940, as Jean claims, then Le Condamné à mort - the real Genet's first published text - would be written subsequently; it was in fact published in 1942. This would seem to confirm that the "writing time" of Miracle implicitly occurs at some remove from Winter 1940.

The power of the well-sung word is made
explicit on the occasion of the adolescent Jean's
arrival at Mettray; he escapes gang rape inflicted
by the tougher boys on condition that he sing.
Accordingly, he intones "Pars," a favourite song
of Nini Buffet, the diseuse whom a drunken Notre-
Dame-des-Fleurs is said to resemble after the drag
ball; Jean's pure clear voice so pleases Villeroy,
the senior boy, that the latter places him under
an exclusive erotic protection. Contiguous in the
text to this reminiscence is an episode at Fontevrault where Jean and Bulkaen's friend Botchako are
discussing the songs particular to reform schools
and also to Fontevrault:

> Le bagne a changé de place
> Son nom a disparu
> Mais on l'a remplacé par une prison
>   immense
> Son nom est Fontevrault
> Ce qui veut dire tombeau...
>   (O.C. II, p. 343)

Botchako is surprised that no songs were composed
by inmates of Mettray; Jean explains to the reader
that Mettray, which has no surrounding wall, does
not retain a sufficient degree of melancholy.
Sadness and nostalgia, on the other hand, are
generated in prisons which have walls, and the emo-
tions bounce against the walls, and reflected back
turn into song. Such an explanation offers parallels with the composition of Genet's own two first
novels, situated in prison and themselves charac-
terised by prevalent motifs of song.

As is the case with Notre-Dame-des-Fleurs,
the writing of Miracle de la Rose represents a certain imaginative liberation of the incarcerated
narrator. For the non-literate prisoner, a paradoxical opportunity to exercise free will is offered
by descent to the Cellule de Punition and Salle de
Discipline; by choosing to commit some additional
fault, an inmate can incur extra punishment. It
seems, however, that few voluntarily descend. As
Dante Ughetti has discerned, "il detenuto, in seno
alla punizione della prigione, e condamnato ad un

ulteriore punizione..." The prisoners tramping
an eternal and infernal round within the Salle
are suffering a double punishment, prison within
prison; the prisoner who deliberately incurs the
double punishment obeys the logic of the double
negative and displays a kind of freedom. By con-
triving to take poison, a beverage not normally
allowed incarcerated persons, Jean earns the additional chastisement, descending to the Cellule
and Salle. It is in the Cellule de Punition that
he claims to have begun *Miracle*:

> ...j'arrivais d'une cellule de puni-
> tion où, pour jouir par les mots du
> souvenir de Bulkaen resté là-haut,
> pour le caresser en caressant les mots
> qui doivent le rappeler à lui en le
> rappelant à moi, j'avais commencé la
> rédaction de ce livre sur les feuilles
> blanches qu'on me remettait pour la
> confection des sacs en papier.
>
> (<u>O.C. II</u>, pp. 253-4)

Some anteceding version of the text would therefore seem to have been undertaken for love of Bulkaen; but it is with Divers that Jean is physically
united in the neighbouring Salle de Discipline,
Divers whom Jean was, at Mettray, in travesty betrothed, Divers whom Jean had for some time failed
to meet at Mettray because, precisely, Divers was
in the equivalent punitive quarters there when Jean
first arrived. Completing the cycle, it is the
belated, successful buggery of Divers which ends
the book.

The destinies of Bulkaen and Harcamone
are prefigured florally by the rose, a motif subject to internal duplication and involving <u>mise en
abyme</u>. In the case of Bulkaen a rapid, partial,
mere suggestion of structural anticipation arises
from an incomplete comparison with one of Ronsard's
"roses:"

> Les cheveux blonds, mais tondus ras,
> les yeux peut-être verts mais certaine-
> ment un regard très dur, le corps souple

> et mince - l'expression qui le
> montrera le mieux: 'la grâce
> dans sa feuille et l'amour se
> repose' - l'air d'avoir vingt
> ans: c'est Bulkaen.
> (<u>O.C. II</u>, p. 235)

Placed in its proper context of the sonnet "Comme
on voit sur la branche, au mois de mai, la rose,"
the quotation would suggest parallels in the destinies of Ronsard's Marie and Genet's Bulkaen:
both will be cut off in their youth, both will be
celebrated by a poet. The quotation is a form of
structural anticipation, since the narration of
the destiny of Pierre, intricately woven into
narration of the destiny of Harcamone, constitutes
only a portion of the total text, itself representing fulfillment of the destiny of Jean.

A more complete prefiguration occurs in
the shaving sequence in which Jean decapitates the
rose. To term this thematic and structural anticipation "metaphorical" might seem unwise at first,
given the difficulty of discerning what is "real"
in the transformation of Harcamone's chains into
roses:

> Harcamone 'm'apparaissait." ... Il
> sortit de cellule. Comme les tourne-
> sols vers le soleil, nos visages se
> tournèrent et pivotèrent nos corps
> sans même que nous nous rendissions
> compte que notre immobilité était
> dérangée... Je sentais, dans toutes
> mes veines, que le miracle était en
> marche. Mais la ferveur de notre ad-
> miration avec la charge de sainteté
> qui pesait sur la chaine serrant ses
> poignets - ses cheveux ayant eu le
> temps de pousser, leurs boucles
> s'embrouillaient sur son front avec
> la cruauté savante de la couronne
> d'épines - firent cette chaine se
> transformer sous nos yeux en une
> guirlande de roses blanches. La

transformation commença au poignet
gauche et continua le long de la
chaine, de maille en maille jusqu'au
poignet droit.
(O.C. II, pp. 233-4)

The comparison "chain - flower - flower - Harcamone" is prepared, vegetably, by the sunflowers:
"Comme les tournesols vers le soleil..." An analogy is then drawn between Harcamone's curls and
a crown of thorns, explicable in terms of visual
similarity, position on the head and parallels in
impending executions: Jesus is distinguished by
his thorns, Harcamone by his hair which, unlike
that of the other prisoners, has been allowed to
grow. A sort of inverted metonymic contiguity -
no thorn without a rose - prepares the reader for
the rose; the garland is justified by implicit
analogy with the drooping loops of chains. What
is problematical is the manner in which this
metaphorical identification becomes a fact of
narrative:

J'avançai de deux pas...les ciseaux
à la main, et je coupai la plus belle
rose qui pendait à une tige souple,
tout près de son poignet gauche. La
tête de la rose tomba sur mon pied
et roula sur le dallage parmi les
boucles de cheveux coupés et sales.
Je la ramassai et relevai mon visage
extasié, assez tôt pour voir
l'horreur peinte sur celui d'Harcamone,
dont la nervosité n'avait pu résister
à la préfiguration si sûre de sa
mort.
(O.C. II, p. 234)

The warders, Jean declares, notice nothing unusual,
which strengthens the reader's first impression
that the transformation takes place entirely in
Jean's imagination; but the act of cutting the
white rose with prison scissors denotes a sudden
fusion of the worlds given as imaginative and real.
It resembles the narrator's metaleptic interven-

tions in <u>Notre-Dame-des-Fleurs</u>, particularly those
involving the motif of false pearls; but in the
first novel the demarcation between frame and secondary narrative is more apparent: Jean is not
a protagonist in the saga of Divine. In <u>Miracle</u>,
Jean's decapitation of the rose is a metalepsis
in the second degree, a fictional transgression
of fiction which reflects the creative meditations
of the novel's ultimate, "present" temporal frame.

The shaving sequence, from imaginative
transformation to metaleptic act, is a structural
metaphor which anticipates and contains in condensed form the imagined "miracle of the rose"
and narrated fact of Harcamone's execution by
guillotine. As such it is remarkably akin to the
phenomenon of <u>mise en abyme</u> as summarily defined
by Gide:

> J'aime assez qu'en une oeuvre
> d'art, on retrouve ainsi transposé,
> à l'échelle des personnages, le
> sujet même de cette oeuvre. Rien
> n'éclaire et n'établit plus sûre-
> ment les proportions de l'ensemble.
> Ainsi, dans les tableaux de Memling
> ou de Quentin Metsys, un petit miroir
> convexe et sombre reflète, à son tour,
> l'intérieure de la scène où se joue
> la scène peinte. Ainsi, dans le
> tableau des ménines de Velasquez
> (mais un peu différemment). Enfin, en
> littérature, dans <u>Hamlet</u>, les scènes
> de marionnettes ou de fête au château.
> Dans la chute de la <u>Maison Usher</u>, la
> lecture que l'on fait à Roderick, etc.[4]

Jean Ricardou, who quotes and develops Gide's indications, dwells on the <u>Maison Usher</u>, adds his own
analysis of <u>Heinrich von Ofterdingen</u> and the Oedipus
myth and concludes that the <u>mise en abyme</u> - as one
might conclude from the term's "vertical" connotations - constitutes a sort of narrative rebellion
against the linear whole:

> ...c'est que la mise en abyme est

avant tout la révolte structurelle
d'un fragment du récit contre l'en-
semble qui le contient.[5]

Not only this, it draws attention to the narrative
act itself:

Dès que le récit se conteste,
il se pose donc aussitôt comme récit,
il évite certain obscurantisme. En
quelque manière il se présente comme
la prise de conscience du récit par
lui-même. Il devient un récit qui,
en se faisant, s'efforce de définir
le fait qu'il y a récit.

Ricardou's masterly commentary on the Oedipus myth
further indicates the interaction between mise en
abyme and narrative: if the Oedipus story contains
three such "revolts," in the form of oracular pre-
dictions, the partial comprehension of the ques-
tioner in each case advances the calamity.

In Miracle, the shaving scene affects,
subtly, both the story told and the telling of the
tale. For one thing, it confirms the narrator in
his self-elected role as Harcamone's mystical betrothed, a confirmation which leads to his spiritual exercises and the eventual miracle. For
another, it underlines the "falseness" or imaginary nature of Jean's narration; one notes that
Jean places the decapitated flower in the false
pocket of his trousers, at the end of the sequence:
"Je mis la rose dans la fausse poche taillée dans
mon froc." Several hundred pages later the stalk
of the same rose is still between Jean's teeth
when, close to completing the cycle, he kisses
Divers.

(c) Literary Affinities: the Romantic

The dualistic properties of Miracle de
la Rose have been both recognised as inherently
Romantic and slightly misconstrued as such. In

his review of the novel, Stephen Koch sets forth
the qualities which justify application of the
term "romantic" to Genet's works, to <u>Miracle de
la Rose</u> in particular:

> Mettray - a former convent, with en-
> circling walls of stone - was Genet's
> mother. Fontevrault penitentiary was
> the arena of his perverse movement into
> manhood. Mettray was Genet's idyll,
> his pastoral; at Fontevrault that idyll
> was ripped to shreds. Genet's whole
> effort in this book is to reassemble
> a shattered and fragmented paradise.
> This is the immemorial motive that lies
> at the center of his art, making of him
> the romantic that he is - the only
> first-rate romantic genius of post-war
> world literature.[6]

Romantic nostalgia, Koch contends, may assume two
basic forms: the flight, in fantasy, from an un-
acceptable present to an ideal past, or the struggle, demonic in its intensity, to overcome that
present by confronting it in a superior spiritual
state. Genet's romanticism - for Koch does not
use the formal generic capital "R" - is of the
latter, actively defiant kind. To contend that
"this is the immemorial motif" lying at the centre
of his art is not, however, to recognise certain
formal properties of that art which suggest other
aspects of Romanticism.

Instances of structural embedding in
German Romanticism, at times barely distinguish-
able from <u>mise en abyme</u>, are enumerated by Lillian
Furst, to the point of seeming narrative essentials
of that movement:

> Again and again throughout German
> Romantic literature a story is told
> within a story: in Novalis' <u>Die
> Lehrlinge zu Sais</u>, the <u>Märchen</u> of
> Hyazinth and Rosenblute is interpo-
> lated into the narrative; similarly
> <u>Heinrich von Ofterdingen</u> is studded

with the tales of the merchants
and of Klingsohr; Tieck's Der
blonde Eckbert contains the story
of Bertha's adventures within
the main story, and in Brentano's
Geschichte vom braven Kasperl und
dem schönern Annerl too, the fate
of the two central characters is
recounted to the narrator by Kasperl's
grandmother...the recurrent preference
for the framework technique surely
reflects the deliberate distancing
of the physical here and now from
the new world created by the imagination: the world within - or
rather beyond - the real world.[7]

The embedded structure of Miracle de la Rose, temporal rather than spatial and hence less readily
discernible than in Notre-Dame-des-Fleurs, does
not correspond exactly to the story told within a
story as indicated by Miss Furst. It is true that
the deaths of Bulkaen and Harcamone are originally
recounted by prison guards, while the episode of
Bulkaen's masochistic enjoyment of humiliation at
Mettray - torture by expectorate - is purportedly
told to Divers who tells it to Jean who then assumes the voice of Bulkaen to narrate it in the
text. That an implicit, embryonic secondary narrative should in each case be reconstructed and re-
told by Jean underlines the importance in Miracle
of the creative imagination. Miss Furst considers
this creative primacy, together with the isolation
implied by the "deliberate distancing" effect of
frames, to be characteristics of Romantic literature.

In Miracle and Notre-Dame, the narrator's
isolation from the world is already suggested by
the locative, incarcerating frame of his cell, from
which both books claim to be written. In Notre-
Dame, this distancing is clearly deliberate: "Le
monde des vivants n'est jamais trop loin de moi.
Je l'éloigne le plus que je peux par tous les moyens
dont je dispose." (O.C. II, p. 114) In Miracle,

although many of the protagonists actively desire
physical freedom - Bulkaen and his friend Botchako
are shot while trying to escape, Harcamone prefers
execution to imprisonment and accordingly murders
a guard to hasten his own end - the narrator resorts to revery and art as means of liberation.
His oneiric escape is made aboard an imaginary
slave-galley, inspired by a ruined hulk at Mettray:

> Mettray prend soudain la place -
> non de la prison que j'habite -
> mais de moi-même, et je m'embarque,
> comme autrefois au fond de mon hamac,
> sur les vestiges de la barque démâtée
> presque détruite, parmi les fleurs du
> Grand Carré, à Mettray. Mon désir de
> fuite et d'amour la camoufle en une
> galère en révolte évadée d'un bagne.
> C'est l'"Offensive." Sur elle, j'ai
> parcouru les mers du Sud, à travers
> les branches, les feuilles, les fleurs
> et les oiseaux de Touraine. A mon
> ordre, la galère foutait le camp.
>   (O.C. II, pp. 286-7)

Many mental motions are condensed into this passage which, incidentally, recalls the poem La
Galère. The galley is a means of flight from
prison into fantasy; that fantasy itself retrieves
the memory of Mettray. Furthermore, the same
fantasy served Jean as a child. That Jean should
narrate past fantasies in this way indicates at
least a retrospective awareness of imaginative
transformation. An alternative instrument of
liberation is provided, paradoxically, by the
"cellule de punition," or solitary confinement,
from which Jean claims to be writing his book. A
prison within a prison, at two removes from the
external world, this disciplinary cell provides
the narrator with the solitude necessary for
literary composition, hence for the realisation
of his destiny.

        The primacy of the creative imagination,
deemed by Miss Furst an essential feature of Romantic art, is made repeatedly manifest in Notre-Dame-

des-Fleurs by transformations both comic and poetic; the prominence of artifice in that work
constantly underlining the parallel existence of
the sublime and the ridiculous. This duality of
vision may be considered a feature of Romantic
art, if one accepts Miss Furst; she comments,
for example, of Novalis:

> The transfiguring force of his imagi-
> nation was brought into play in his
> early encounter with Sophie von Kühn;
> rationally he could accept the limi-
> tations of this thirteen-year-old,
> even complaining that poetry interes-
> ted her not a whit...yet he did -
> admittedly after her death - idealise
> her to an unprecedented degree.[8]

In Miracle de la Rose, the transfiguring power of
Genet's imagination is most conspicuously displayed
in his depiction of the death of Harcamone. On
the night of the execution, Jean and Divers have
been making love; Divers falls asleep, leaving Jean
awake, smoking cigarette ends. Despite a vast
fatigue, Jean continues his elucubrations on behalf
of Harcamone - "mon activité de voyante et d'ascète"
- whom he is determined to assist by every spiritual
means available. In the narrator's imagination,
four men dressed in black - judge, lawyer, almoner
and executioner - wake Harcamone in his cell. The
condemned man is then transformed into a gigantic
figure who bursts through the cell walls and fills
the universe:

> Sans changer d'un pouce, il devint
> immense, dépassant la cellule qu'il
> creva, emplit l'univers et les quatre
> hommes noirs rapetissèrent jusqu'à
> n'être pas plus gros que quatre
> punaises.
>   (O.C. II, p. 462)

This vast but static enlargement once effected, the
four shrunken men of law enter Harcamone through
the ear and mouth - one thinks of the sixth pilgrim
in Gargantua - and proceed to explore a complex but

desolate interior, compared by Jean to a sort of
tortuous Toulon. Empowered by his cerebral efforts
to attend the search for the heart of Harcamone,
Jean is permitted to behold the miraculous centre
of the rose, itself encased, characteristically,
within a double chamber:

> Mais à peine l'un des quatre eut-il
> pensé qu'ils n'étaient pas au coeur
> du coeur, qu'une porte s'ouvrit
> d'elle-même, et nous nous trouvâmes
> en face d'une rose rouge, monstrueuse
> de taille et de beauté.
> -La Rose Mystique, murmura
>   l'aumonier.
>
> (<u>O.C. II</u>, p. 464)

Stumbling forward in eager profanation, the four
funereal figures separate the petals and reveal
the heart of the rose to be a dark vertiginous
hole; seized with dizziness, they pitch into the
void.

Characteristically, the execution scene -
or rather, the miracle of the rose which represents
Jean's transfiguration of the execution he relates -
is preceded by an explanation of how the fantasy
occurred:

> Je fus tout à coup touché par
> l'odeur des roses et mes yeux
> furent emplis par la vue de la
> glycine de Mettray... A peine
> ce souvenir des fleurs m'eut-il
> visité que se précipitèrent aux
> yeux de mon esprit les scènes que
> je vais dire.
>
> (<u>O.C. II</u>, p. 461)

That Jean should bother to relate, as a part of
the narrative, the mnemonic origin of his fantasy
indicated once again his concern with imaginative
processes and the creative act. This very concern
implies duality, involving a simultaneous awareness
of the transformable and the transformed. Manifest, therefore, as a self-conscious literary per-

spective imposed on narrated events, Genet's use
of the frame in <u>Miracle de la Rose</u> may be said to
resemble the German Romantics' use of that device
in the emphasis it places on imaginative power
and in the distance it implies between the imagination and the world.

Simply to conclude from this that Genet
is Romantic would nonetheless be risky and somewhat arbitrary. Duality in <u>Miracle</u> amounts to
more than what might be called, somewhat metaphysically and metatextually, the author's imagination.
Complex temporal conventions which draw attention
to the act of writing as a fictional theme, internal duplication of thematic and structural motifs,
<u>mise en abyme</u> - all combine to anticipate, if
not the actual New Novel, at least an awareness
of certain problems later raised by that phenomenon: most notably, the idea of narration as a
subject of itself.

NOTES TO CHAPTER III

[1]Dante Ughetti, "Motivi orfifi nel Miracle de la Rose," Biblioteca del Archivum Romanicum, 89-91 (I-1967), p. 46.

[2]Gérard Genette, Figures III (Paris: Seuil, 1972), p. 229.

[3]Figures III, p. 231.

[4]Gide, Journal 1893 (sic), quoted by Jean Ricardou in his Problèmes du nouveau roman (Paris: Seuil, 1967), pp. 172-3.

[5]Ricardou, p. 181.

[6]Stephen Koch, "The Romantic of the Wretched Life," Nation 204 (June 12, 1967), p. 763.

[7]Lillian R. Furst, Romanticism in Perspective (London: Macmillan, 1969), pp. 200-201.

[8]Furst, p. 201.

CHAPTER IV: POMPES FUNEBRES

(a) Structure and Metaphor

        Pronouncing upon the merits and failures
of Pompes funèbres, the English critic Philip Thody
deems it the worst of Genet's novels, lacking in
structural cohesion, unable to offset its "general
air of unreality" and "self-indulgent rhetoric"
with a sufficient number of credible passages.
Yet Thody does concede that the book may appeal
to readers "who, like Cocteau, place the highest
value on the surrealist and irrational aspects
of his work.[1] Genet's third novel, Pompes funèbres is his first published work not claiming
composition in a prison cell. It nonetheless
incorporates certain structural and metaphorical
quintessentials of preceding tomes.

        In a sense, to read Pompes funèbres is
to enter Genet's chamber of funereal horrors. The
novel, which is set in the Paris of the Liberation, is dedicated to Jean Decarnin, a young com-
munist Resistance fighter killed at the barricades
in August 1944. In actual life Jean Decarnin was
Genet's lover, a fact incidentally responsible
for the imprisonment from which Sartre and Cocteau
wrested Genet; Jean had committed a crime for
which the poet assumed responsibility.[2] Like
Pilorge in Notre-Dame-des-Fleurs, Jean Decarnin
possesses two identities, for he is also the
narrator "Jean Genet's" innamorato and Pompes
funèbres is his memorial, in fiction and in fact.
Again like Notre-Dame-des-Fleurs the book opens,
as it were, by means of a newspaper:

        Les journaux qui parurent à
        la Libération de Paris, en août
        1944, dirent assez ce que furent
        ces journées d'héroïsme puéril,
        quand le corps fumait de bravoure
        et d'audace... Des photographies
        montrent encore des cadavres
        dépecés, mutilés, et les villages
        en ruine, Oradour et Montsauche, in-
        cendiés par les soldats allemands.
        C'est à l'intérieur de cette tragédie

> que se place l'événement: la
> mort de Jean D. qui donne
> prétexte à ce livre.
> (O.C. III, p. 9)

Grisly images persist throughout, whether presented as fantastic or as "real."   In his unconsola-
ble grief "Jean Genet" dreams of sodomising his
dead friend, realising that the fantasy involves
a form of necrophilia; towards the novel's end,
he imagines himself devouring Jean with full culi-
nary ceremony and tam-tams beating an accompaniment.   Besides these melancholic excesses, the
narrative boasts several murders, Riton's des-
patching of the cat, scenes of torture on the
Russian front, glimpses into the professional
duties of a Berlin executioner, a "massacre of
innocents," at least two rapes, an account of the
menstruation of Joan of Arc, and fantasies concerning Hitler's genitalia.   Furthermore, the work
seems conceived as a metaphor for sodomy, a slow
penetration into blackness corresponding to the
narrator's defloration of his friend.   These eccentricities are to a mild degree announced in
the indecent titular pun, the word "pompes" being
translatable as "rites" but also "pumps," or even
"sucks," with inevitable sexual connotations.

        In addition to peculiarities of content,
Pompes funèbres is extremely hard to read, at
least in the commercial edition of 1953.   Apparently appalled by Genet's treatment of the theme of
treason, Gallimard has excised from the 1947 version a variety of passages amounting to at least
thirty pages.   The structure of the novel is such
that these cuts constitute a severe menace to its
continuity and comprehensibility.   Like Miracle de
la Rose, Pompes funèbres is apparently written by
a narrator recalling past events in which he par-
ticipated.   The narrating "Genet," though not
actually incarcerated on this occasion, does claim
to be writing from a suitably isolated retreat
near a monastery.   Once again, the frame concerns
the writing of the novel, while the secondary or
inner narrative - as in Notre-Dame-des-Fleurs -

relates the mostly amorous deeds of the protagonists as imaginatively reconstructed by the narrator. To a greater extent, though, than in <u>Notre-
Dame</u>, fact and fantasy combine in <u>Pompes funèbres</u>,
acting as catalysts in the technical experiments
with form. They are brought together by the surrealistic ineluctable of chance: fortuitous creation
of characters, coincidence, chance encounters of
those characters. Chance is treated as an instrument of destiny, hence as a fictional theme; it is
appropriated as a creative method, a means of composing the book. Its function is thus double, at
once structural and thematic.

As in the two preceding novels, three
major temporal levels coexist throughout to constitute the book's apparently chaotic chronology: an
absolute present, or "writing time," in which the
narrator Jean Genet speaks of himself, his novel,
and his current fantasies concerning his dead
friend; a recent past, which one might call "August
1944," encompassing events real and imaginary before
and after Jean Decarnin's death, proceeding up to
the unspecified moment when Jean Genet starts to
write; and flashbacks, imagined by the narrator,
which embrace the supposed adolescence of his
characters. Owing to the complicated functioning
of chance as a structuring agent, it occasionally
seems that the narrator's temporal situation is
intercalated between the events he describes; yet
the overall temporal logic of the book would seem
to deny this impression. Additional obstacles to
comprehension result from the double functions of
the protagonists, most of whom exist in contexts
given both as real and imaginary. As in <u>Miracle
de la Rose</u>, Jean Genet is actively involved with
these dual personnages, and his own narrating "je"
designates both agent and narrator.

Following the newspaper quotations which
open the book, establish the scene of action and,
in some degree, generate the narrative, the story
of "August 1944" begins abruptly with the statement
"Quand je revins de la Morgue... il faisait nuit,"
(<u>O.C. III</u>, p. 9) thereby establishing a reference

point in time shortly after Jean Decarnin's death.
The narrator then meditates for about a page, in
his absolute but unspecified present, about the
manner of his novel's composition. This meditation
leads him to recall a series of visits paid to
Jean's mother in her apartment in Paris. In the
course of these "condolences," the chronology of
which is deliberately upset, "Genet" meets Erik
Seiler, a German tank driver who, left behind in
the Axis retreat, is hiding in Mme Decarnin's
house and has become her lover. Interjected between visits are descriptions of Jean's funeral,
an account of the narrator's pilgrimmage to the
spot where Jean was killed, and a series of
imaginary reconstructions - again, out of chronological sequence - of Erik's adolescence as a member of the Hitler Youth. In the course of these
activities, "Genet" also meets Paulo, Jean's half-
brother, for whom he likewise refashions an imaginary past; all these fantasies contribute to the
action of the inner narrative. Distressed by his
first encounter with Paulo, "Genet" takes refuge
in a cinema, which happens to be showing newsreels
of the fighting on the roofs. Amid howls of de-
rision, there appears on the screen the haggard
face of an adolescent militiaman - that is, a
member of a detested armed force of collaborating
Frenchmen. Paradoxically attracted to the youth
by the intensity of his own hatred, the narrator
spontaneously baptises him "Riton;" to exorcise
his own pain, he further decides to imagine that
it was Riton who shot down Jean Decarnin. The
decision affords him vast relief, for it accounts -
again in the narrator's imagination - for the
immediate past of Erik:

> Je venais de découvrir comment et
> auprès de qui Erik avait passé les
> cinq premiers jours de la révolte
> de Paris avant de pouvoir se planquer
> chez sa maitresse. Riton rencontrera
> Erik, combattra près de lui sur les
> toits, mais avant cela il fallait
> qu'il connût Paulo.
> (O.C. III, p. 39)

The original edition obligingly makes clear that
Paulo, having been successively rejected by the
French Gestapo, the Resistance and the Militia,
had been reduced to burglary in company with
Riton. But Riton is an "invented" character,
taken from the newsreel by the narrator, and then
introduced into the lives of Paulo and Erik as
the narrator imagines them. Those events depicted
as "real" - Jean Genet's business with Decarnin's
family - are thus inextricably entangled in his
fantasies. "Genet's" imagination oscillates between the actual and the imaginary, self-consciously
welding the two into a novel. This dialectic multiplicity is once again reflected in the title.
Not only are the "pompes funèbres" the ceremonial
rites of Jean Decarnin's burial, as described in
the book; they are also the erotic imaginings of
"Jean Genet." They are the romantic liaisons of
his characters, which constitute a part of those
imaginings, and the novel itself, written as a
testimonial expulsion of his grief.

        Having found a rooftop partner for Erik
and having established links between his half-
imaginary personnages, "Genet" proceeds with what
now becomes the main thrust of his narrative: the
love-affair between Erik and Riton. To reconstruct
even this, the narrator must plunge back months
and years in time, indicating how Riton, through
hunger, was led to join the Militia; how he first
met Erik; how, later, in the combat on the roofs
he met Erik again, there to enjoy a brief catamitic
idyll. The story of Erik and Riton - itself far
from sequent - is constantly interrupted by flashbacks to "Jean Genet's" acts of love with Jean
Decarnin, by fantasies concerning Hitler, who
enters the story rather implausibly as Paulo's
associate in buggery, and by additional reflections
on the military, amorous and murderous career of
Erik Seiler. A further complication for the reader
is that the narrator often identifies with his
characters, slipping "inside" Riton, Erik and Hitler by means of the subjective "je": of Erik, for
example, he observes:

Dès la première fois que je le vis,
au sortir de l'appartement, je m'ef-
forçai de remonter le courant de sa
vie et, pour plus d'efficacité, je
rentrai dans son uniforme, dans ses
bottes, dans sa peau... j'avais dix-
huit ans, jeune hitlérien de garde
dans le jardin, où j'étais assis au
pied d'un arbre.
                        (O.C. III, pp. 24-5)

This transgressive identification with Erik, a
sort of personal narratorial metalepsis, corresponds on one level to the mental exercises Genet
the character might perform, the better to under-
stand a new friend. On another level, it underlines the illusory nature of character creation.
Characters being necessarily a product of their
author, an attempt on the part of the narrating
"author" to enter into their heads constitutes an
artificial inversion of the actual procedure.

The concatenation on fantasies which
constitutes the book is brought to an end when
Riton and Erik, trapped on the roof and expecting
any minute to be killed, eventually drop their
trousers and make love: "Le dos appuyé au monument
de briques, en face de Paris qui veillait, Erik
encula Riton." (O.C. III, p. 158)   The sodomy performed, Riton takes up a machine-gun and shoots
his blond friend. His reasons for so doing are
left unexplained; one may suppose an access of joy
which will not permit of banal post-coital senti-
ments, or perhaps a desire to preserve Erik from
the liberating French. At all events, this final
murder is a symmetric complement to the narrator's
own bereavement. The ending is nonetheless curious,
for being deliberately false, despite the minute
and uncomfortable realism of the descriptions which
precede it. "Je venais de découvrir comment et
auprès de qui Erik avait passé les cinq premiers
jours de la révolte... avant de pouvoir se planquer
chez sa maitresse," writes the narrator, at the
inception of his exorcism; yet, by the nature of
the exercise, Erik would logically be dead at the

time of their first meeting. In effect, the novel's
mortal termination either negates the meetings in
Mme Decarnin's apartment, or it confirms the unreality of the entire sequence between Erik and
Riton. It would seem that the real and the unreal
simply coexist in fiction, concomitant necessities
in the narrator's mind.

    The workings of contraption and coinci-
dence may be observed in the fantastical encounters
which determine the pattern of the novel's rudimentary plot. These encounters, presented as hapha-
sard, in fact result from an intricate series of
associations and digressions. When first "Genet"
meets Erik, the latter is seated in a manner which,
"Genet" cannot help but think, must cause an intimate obstruction: "Je ne sais quoi provoqua en moi
l'éclosion de cette idée qu'il gênait, d'être assis
sur une chaise de paille, son oeil de Gabès." (O.
C. III, p. 14) In an inevitable sequence of association, the narrator recalls a scene - whether real
or imaginary is not clear - in which a bataillon-
naire entertained three boys with an anal anecdote
while ascending the vertiginous rue des Martyrs.
It appears, in the original edition of Pompes
funèbres, that one of these three youths was called
Pierrot. This same Pierrot later "betrays" twenty-
eight adolescent innocents suspected of being in-
surgents in a penal revolt. The boys are sentenced
to be shot, and Riton, it happens, now in the
Militia, is assigned to the firing-squad. After
the butchery, the desperately shaken executioners
are given Sunday off. Returning to the barracks
after a miserable day of drunkenness, Riton meets
Erik in the crowded métro, his buttocks being
squashed against the latter's virile parts in a
comic anticipation of their eventual union. Their
meeting is both a necessary requirement of the plot
- whose function, after all, is to permit the
narrator a full attainment of his destiny - and
the necessary outcome of associative ideas. It is
a product of the narrator's desire to exorcise the
horror of Jean's death with a literary glut of
things macabre - death, sodomy and evil. Because
the chronology of their subsequent meetings is up-

set, the pattern of their encounters does appear to follow the dictates of the narrator's revery, while being incorporated into his deliberate aims.

    While <u>Notre-Dame-des-Fleurs</u> - to which Genet incidentally compares <u>Pompes funèbres</u>, in the opening pages of the latter - is critically held to be the more successful novel, it does not equal <u>Pompes funèbres</u> in the absorption of plot into metaphor. If <u>Notre-Dame-des-Fleurs</u> opens with the structural metaphor of photographic frames, this metaphor is nonetheless unrelated to the title. In the case of <u>Pompes funèbres</u>, however, the multiple, obscene associations of the title are metaphorically apparent throughout the work; episode after episode is resolved in a sexual image. Dominating the entire work is the narrator's vision of the "oeil de bronze," that ultimate male favour with which the narrator, in his memories of Jean, seems obsessed. Even as he enters the church for his lover's funeral, the "oeil" presents itself to "Genet" as a natural simile for the edifice's orificial darkness: "Il y fait noir comme dans le trou du cul d'un nègre." (<u>O.C. III</u>, p. 11) Allied to this obsequial obscenity are the sempiternal themes of love and death, themes which, throughout the novel, are closely intertwined: "Genet's" erotic reveries concerning Jean cannot be separated from the latter's decease; Paulo, while sodomising Hitler, is convinced he faces execution for that privilege. When the Berlin executioner penetrates young Erik in the park, the former's professional capacity naturally connotes violent death. Jean's fiancée is raped by gravediggers at the burial of her bastard daughter - a variation, perhaps, on the Romantic theme of Death and the Maiden; Riton is raped by a German soldier whose nerves are exacerbated by impending death; Riton, having "impaled himself" on Erik's member, shoots his friend immediately after making love. Beyond the thematic equivalence of love and death, a somewhat gruesome metaphorical identification of anus and extinction is established by these grisly repetitions.

(b) Contacts with Surrealism

Genet's historical contacts with the Surrealist movement exist, but in a somewhat questionable form. One thinks of his encounters with Cocteau, a writer who may be said to have anticipated, in his youth, certain surrealist procedures and themes; but Cocteau was detested by the group - in fact, Breton found him quite abominable. Sartre relates that the Surrealists energetically rejected Genet himself, appalled by his eulogies of treason.[3] One suspects that Breton, always rather high-minded about love, was probably also repelled by Genet's homosexuality. Be that as it may, Genet is known to have had "surrealistic" contacts in Paris after the war, with Breton himself and the painter Leonor Fini.[4]

Despite an evident ideological disconnection and a vast disparity in subject-matter - Breton's unusual, indeed mad heroine being antipodal to Genet's feline killer Riton - initial paragraphs of, for example, Nadja and of Pompes funèbres do present some curious analogies. Nadja, Breton states, is a random composition which reveals its author to be the object of his own sub-conscious, a pawn of his own destiny:

> Je me bornerai ici à me souvenir
> sans effort de ce qui, ne répondant
> à aucune démarche de ma part, m'est
> quelquefois advenu, de ce qui me
> donne, m'arrivant par des voies in-
> soupçonnables, la mesure de la grâce
> et de la disgrâce particulière dont
> je suis l'objet; j'en parlerai sans
> ordre pré-établi, et selon le caprice
> de l'heure qui laisse surnager ce
> qui surnage.[5]

Breton then informs the reader that he is writing Nadja from the Manoir d'Ango at Varengeville-sur-Mer: "Etait-il possible qu'il en fût autrement, dès lors que je voulais écrire Nadja?" Despite the naive marvel of the tone, therefore, Nadja is to some extent a willed creation. In a comparable

paragraph of <u>Pompes funèbres</u>, the narrator sets
forth his aims in a long paragraph which betrays
an obsessive perplexity at the workings of his
literary destiny:

> Je ne m'attacherai jamais assez
> aux conditions dans lesquelles j'écris
> ce livre. S'il est vrai qu'il a pour
> but avoué de dire la gloire de Jean D.
> il a peut-être des buts seconds plus
> imprévisibles. Ecrire, c'est choisir
> l'un entre les dix matériaux qui vous
> sont proposés. Je me demande pourquoi
> j'ai accepté de fixer par les mots tel
> fait plutôt qu'un autre d'égale impor-
> tance. Pourquoi suis-je limité dans
> mon choix et me vois-je dépeindre
> bientôt le troisième enterrement de
> mes trois livres?
> (<u>O.C. III</u>, p. 10)

The surrealist concept of the sub-conscious as a
creative agent surfaces in the hint of unforeseeable
literary ends - "des buts...imprévisibles" - while
the very acceptance of "j'ai accepté de fixer..."
implies a degree of passivity. Yet Genet is both
behind and beyond the Surrealists; passivity and
acceptance are vestigial, and the narrator must
needs question them. His interrogation, retrospective and quasi-analytical, recalls the morbid
obsessions of <u>Marche funèbre</u>, a poem recalled also
by titular echo; in <u>Pompes funèbres</u>, however, the
poetical preoccupation with the theme of death is
succeeded by the troubling recurrence of the funeral
rites. Long before he knew Jean Decarnin, the
narrator records, he had "chosen" words describing
the funeral of Jean's purported bastard, which obsequies are found in <u>Pompes funèbres</u>. It would
further seem that the narrator in some way connects
Divine's funeral, in <u>Notre-Dame-des-Fleurs</u>, with
the death of Jean:

> Il est troublant qu'un thème macabre
> m'ait été offert il y a longtemps,
> afin que je le traite aujourd'hui et
> l'incorpore malgré moi à un texte

124

> chargé de décomposer le rayon
> lumineux, fait surtout d'amour et
> de douleur, que projette mon coeur
> désolé. J'écris ce livre auprès
> d'un monastère élevé tout droit au
> milieu des forêts, dans les rochers
> et les ronces. Le long du torrent,
> j'aime revivre les angoisses d'Erik,
> le beau tankiste boche, de Paulo, de
> Riton. J'écrirai sans précautions.
> Mais j'insiste encore sur l'étrangeté
> de ce destin qui me fit décrire au
> début de <u>Notre-Dame-des-Fleurs</u> un
> enterrement que j'allais mener selon
> les pompes secrètes du coeur et de
> l'esprit, deux ans après.
> (<u>O.C. III</u>, p. 10)

The retreat which the narrator has chosen for the
task of composition is classically Romantic; it
could have served as a setting for a <u>Marchenroman</u>
or, alternatively, one of Julien Gracq's post-
surrealist novels. It has, however, scant further
function in the tale. When the narrator declares
"j'écrirai sans précautions," he seems almost to
echo Breton's "j'en parlerai sans order pré-
établi"; yet Genet uses random composition in a
far more complex manner than does Breton. The
theme of literary destiny is inseparable both from
"Genet's" conscious aims - the celebration of the
dead beloved - and from the presumably autonomous
machinations which cause the burial theme so to
re-appear. No doubt this funereal coincidence
troubles the narrator precisely in its implication
of both life and art; if, in his art, the recurrence of obsequies is explicable as a surfacing
obsession, it is one which appears peculiarly
attuned to the existential governance of destiny.
In involving the creative act in this strange interaction of fate and the psyche, Genet goes a
step further than Breton, who affects to remain
the passive agent of his sub-conscious.

It is perhaps pertinent to quote, in
conclusion, a comment passed in 1960 on a vastly

different post-surrealist novel, Julien Gracq's
Un Balcon en forêt of 1960:

> ...ce thème (de la guerre), s'il
> garde la marque de l'histoire n'en
> est pas moins transposé dans le
> mythe car l'auteur reconnait le pré-
> existence d'une unité de l'homme
> et du destin. C'est une hypothèse
> que les surréalistes trouvèrent
> déjà formulée à l'état d'affirmation
> sous la plume des romantiques alle-
> mands. Dans Un Balcon en forêt, la
> guerre mondiale n'apparait plus comme
> une donnée objective susceptible
> d'être rangée dans une catégorie
> rationnelle mais elle entoure d'un
> cercle magique l'existence de l'homme
> et de la Nature. Au-delà de la
> personne et de l'esprit, l'événement
> historique est intimement lié au
> royaume des songes.[6]

The existence of Nature must obviously be discarded
in a discussion of the war-torn, Parisian setting
of Pompes funèbres, and Julien Gracq's atmosphere
of delicate unreality cannot be said to resemble
Genet's anilingual fantasies. Nor is Genet's use
of war exactly similar, although it does form an
historical background, and the narrator's Hitlerian
indulgences do represent an attempt to elevate his
personal obsessions with sodomy and death to a more
grandiose scale of perpetrated evil. Yet Genet's
interrogation of the chance events which so en-
tangle art and life in funeral rites - with all the
connotations we have seen - almost amounts to a
recognition of a pre-existing unification with his
private destiny. In Genet's case, that destiny is
realised through the writing of his novel.

        In its identification of fate, coinci-
dence, and the narrator's preconceptions of the
same - in other words, in its metaphysical fusion
of the subject and the object - Pompes funèbres
is therefore comparable to at least one product
of neo-surrealism. One may further say that a

distinct affinity is apparent between Genet's
visually-oriented eroticism and the concatenations
of erotic images which characterise much surrealist
painting, most notably perhaps the onanistic iconog-
raphy of Dali.[7] When, for example, early in Pompes
funèbres the narrator's distraught and grieving mind
deforms and confuses two remarks by Mme Decarnin,
the resultant jumbled phrase "Vous vous exposez au
milieu des bougies" conjures up a series of related
images themselves pertaining to the book's essential themes; the words "vous vous exposez" suggest
exposure both of the narrator's grief and his person, while the "bougies" which Mme Decarnin is
arranging have phallic and funereal connotations.
When, at Jean's internment, the narrator equates
the darkness of the nave with negroid orifice, the
associations are again visually erotic, and might
well have sprung from an anti-clerical vein of
Dali's "paranoiac" imagination. Even Genet's or-
nate and impeccable rhetoric, a sort of literary
equivalent to the elegant perfections he notes in
Leonor Fini's painting,[8] may be compared in some
measure to the sumptuous surfaces of Dali's work,
with the technical mastery of his "academic" surrealism. Taking into account the fact that Genet's
social contacts with Surrealists and quasi-surreal-
ists were made in the period of the movement's
decline, and given his own unconcern with specifically Surrealist doctrine, it is no doubt wiser to
avoid terming him Surrealist in the stricter senses
of the word. Pompes funèbres is, rather, the work
of a neo-surrealist of strong erotico-visual
persuasion.

NOTES TO CHAPTER IV

[1] Philip Thody, <u>Jean Genet</u> (London: Hamish Hamilton, 1968), p. 118.

[2] The circumstance is mentioned in the editorial letter of <u>Combat</u>, July 16, 1948, which Sartre and Cocteau addressed to President Auriol.

[3] ...dans le concert de clameurs qu'a provoqué l'apologie de la trahison publiée par Genet dans <u>Les Temps Modernes</u>, ce sont les surréalistes qui ont crié le plus fort. Ils condamnaient déjà sa pédérastie, les voici outrés par ses délations. Sartre, <u>Saint-Genet</u> (Paris: Gallimard, 1952), p. 196.

[4] "Bagarres littéraires au petit restaurant de la rue des Canettes. Mme Fouchet, la mère de Max-Pol, s'aperçoit que tout est inondé de sang. Le patron explique qu'un nègre qui accompagnait Jean Genêt (sic) lui a porté un coup qui était destiné à la partie postérieure de son individu mais qui l'a profondément atteint à la cuisse. André Breton, qui se trouvait là, aurait essayé de calmer les adversaires mais aurait été blessé également. Bébé Bérard que je rencontre le soir - hier soir - chez Marie Laure, au cours d'un grand diner, a une version différente. Comme dit Max-Pol, je préfère le coup de revolver de Rimbaud.

...Max-Pol qui est venu déjeuner, rectifie l'histoire du coup de poignard de Jean Genêt. C'est la suite d'une longue histoire. Un charmant garçon qui l'accompagnait a reçu le coup de couteau destiné à une artère de la cuisse de J.G. et porté par un nègre de la Rose rouge. Mais Breton là-dessus palabrant! Ah! Nous sommes, malgré tout, fort loin de Verlaine-Rimbaud et de François Villon."

Lise Deharme, <u>Les Années perdues</u> (<u>journal 1939-49</u>) (Paris: Plon, 1961), pp. 251-4. Mme

Deharme, Christian Bérard, etc., were all friends of Leonor Fini.

[5] Nadja (Paris: Gallimard, 1928), p. 25.

[6] Gerda Zeltner, La Grande Aventure du roman au XXe. siècle (Paris: Editions Gonthier, 1967), pp. 131-2.

[7] The similarities between Genet and Dali are not suggested, as one might suppose, by the thesis of Eugene Alesch, which confines itself to Genet's theatre and is primarily concerned with use of space. One might, however, wish to pursue analogies between Genet's third novel and the medium of film. As has been pointed out in the doctoral thesis of Barbara Gerber (Diss; Univ; Wisconsin, pp. 37-8), Genet's use of montage and flashback, in all his novels, is distinctly cinematic. As far as Dali is concerned, however, one wonders if a particular motif from Notre-Dame-des-Fleurs and Miracle de la Rose might not have been suggested by the famous slitting of the eye in the Bunuel-Dali film Un Chien andalou. It is a motif with which Genet almost seems obsessed; in Notre-Dame, Divine's boyhood lover Alberto dies after a brawl in which his left eye is torn out: "Alberto eut l'oeil gauche arraché." (O.C. II, p. 180) In Miracle, the narrator relates how he was sent to Mettray: "...ma cruauté de seize ans voulut que je crevasse l'oeil gauche à un enfant..." (O.C. II, p. 405) Whether the incident is truly from Genet's past is unfortunately a matter for speculation. (The left eye is slit in Bunuel's memorable image.)

[8] See his Lettre à Leonor Fini (Paris: J. Loyau, 1950), unpaginated.

CHAPTER V: THE DRAMATIST

(a) Introduction: Dual Structures in the Plays

        "Il vous faut donc une présentation,"
wrote Genet to J.-J. Pauvert, current publisher
of his play Les Bonnes, in 1954: "...mais c'est
plutôt du théâtre en général que je voudrais dire
quelques mots. Je ne l'aime pas."[1] In view of
this flat avowal, it is a curious paradox that
Genet's plays, far more than his novels, verse or
essays, have established his literary reputation
in Europe and America. As early as 1947, J.-J.
Riniéri observed, of Les Bonnes: "Or voici qu'il
aborde le théâtre, avec une pièce d'une étrange
et rare violence...qui révèle un tempérament
dramatique singulier... (et) qui force à repenser
...le problème du théâtre."[2] More recently,
Lucien Goldmann has termed Genet "un très grand
auteur réaliste," comparable to Brecht: "Qu'il
l'ait voulu ou non," he writes of Le Balcon, "et
avec une vision du monde tout à fait différente,
Genet a écrit la première grande pièce Brechtienne
de la littérature française."[3] The otherwise hos-
tile Catholic critic, Pierre de Boisdeffre, has
opined of Genet's plays: "Ici s'exprime un amateur de théâtre d'une exceptionnelle intelligence,"
adding that the "Préface des Bonnes" - presumably
this same prolegomenon A Pauvert - is as worthy
of inclusion in theatrical anthologies as Artaud's
Théâtre et son double.[4] It is a further irony
that the general disdain which Genet manifests for
occidental drama should apparently have fostered
the theoretical writings - most notably, A Pauvert
- which constitute a significant aspect of his
dramaturgy.

        Apart from those dramatic fragments re-
portedly lost or destroyed in fits of rage -
Splendid's, Le Bagne, Elle[5] - Genet has written
five published plays: Haute Surveillance, Les
Bonnes, Le Balcon, Les Nègres and Les Paravents.
All have been performed, with varying degrees of
scandal and success. All, to a greater or lesser
degree, embody the theatrical concept expressed,
embryonically, in A Pauvert:

> Je ne sais ce que sera le théâtre
> dans un monde socialiste, je com-
> prends mieux ce qu'il serait chez
> les Mau-Mau, mais dans le monde
> occidental, de plus en plus touché
> par la mort et tourné vers elle il
> ne peut que raffiner dans la
> "réflexion" de comédie de comédie,
> de reflet de reflet qu'un jeu
> cérémonieux pourrait rendre
> exquis et proche de l'invisibilité.[6]

All, except for Haute Surveillance, contain elements of "play within a play," the dramatic equivalent of the dual structuring or narrative embedding apparent in the first three novels. Even
Haute Surveillance, however, possesses thematic
and structural elements which connect it with preceding and subsequent works.

Though presumably written in 1946 Genet's
first play, Haute Surveillance or Deathwatch as it
is known in English, was not performed until 1949.
Like Miracle de la Rose, Haute Surveillance is set
in prison; like Sartre's Huis-Clos of 1944, it has
a cast of three, with occasional interruptions
from a fourth character, a guard. Of the three
convicts in Genet's play, Yeux-Verts is a prestigious
criminal awaiting trial for murder; Maurice is a
young thug apparently destined for a future of
splendiferous misdeeds; Lefranc is a less gifted
miscreant who nonetheless aspires to criminal renown. An offstage character, the Negro murderer
Snowball, dominates the action much as Harcamone
dominated Fontevrault in Miracle de la Rose. The
most Sartrian of Genet's dramas, Haute Surveillance
resembles Huis-Clos structurally and thematically:
Lefranc's efforts to impose his concept of himself
upon the other two recall the infernal problem of
autrui as posed in Sartre's play. Frustrated and
tantalised, Lefranc is eventually reduced to mur-
dering Maurice, a deed which brings him not the
desired esteem of Yeux-Verts but disdain, and utter
moral solitude. As Yeux-Verts explains, a great
crime cannot be willed, but descends like a gift

from the gods. If the ritual violence of the murder of Maurice seems to imply the influence of
Artaud, Haute Surveillance has also been termed
"classical" by virtue of its metaphysical intensity. Critics have compared the destinies of Genet's
thugs to the downfalls of the monarchs of Racine;
other critics have seen the play as a solemn parody
of Jansenistic Grace and Will.[7] Yeux-verts, the
murderer who did not wish his crime, is seen in
the latter view as a recipient of inverted grace,
of true criminality. Lefranc, who wills his act,
acquires not criminal prestige but opprobrium.
Yet the termination is both peripatetic and ambiguous; scorned by Yeux-verts, Lefranc unintentionally
attains to the killer's true estate of solitude,
thereby implying that Grace is irresistible and
human will is nought. It is, however, the more
Sartrian theme of identity, identity as reflected
in the opinions of others, which connects Haute
Surveillance with Genet's later plays.

Genet's second play, Les Bonnes, again
presents a quest for identity through crime - or,
as Goldmann would say, for authenticity. Once a-
gain, the cast is limited to three: two incestuous
maids, Claire and Solange Lemercier, and their employer, known simply as Madame. No fourth person
intrudes, though the offstage "Monsieur," Madame's
sponsor and lover, dominates the play's intimate
hierarchies as did Snowball in Haute Surveillance.
In Les Bonnes, however, Genet introduces the deliberate use of a double theatrical illusion which
marks his personal dramatic style. When the curtain rises, Claire and Solange are in mid-imperso-
nation: Solange as Claire, Claire as Madame.
This duplicity becomes definitively clear to the
audience when the maids' secret ritual - which is
supposed to culminate in the symbolic murder of
Madame - is interrupted by an alarm-clock, set to
warn them of Madame's impending return. The ritual,
it transpires, is an habitual one, which habitually
fails, but on this occasion, the maids' sordid rou-
tine of frustration and fantasy has acquired a new
dimension: Solange has brought false, anonymous
charges against Monsieur, who is being held by the

police. But the plot backfires. Monsieur is set
free, telephones, and leaves a message for Madame.
It is clear that the false accusations will be
traced to Claire and Solange, who thus face imminent incomprehension and disgrace. They resolve
once again to kill Madame with poisoned tea. Madame herself then returns, delivers herself of
some histrionic professions of devotion to Monsieur,
learns fortuitously of his liberty and leaves to
meet him in a café. At this juncture the fantasy
which Claire and Solange have so often partially
enacted is brought to its logical conclusion;
fully to realise their identity, they must become
the "eternal couple of the criminal and the saint."
Claire again assumes the role of Madame, dictating
to Solange to serve the poisoned lime tea destined
for Madame. The action of the play thus involves
a motion from illusion - Claire acting Madame,
Solange acting Claire - to reality, or rather,
realisation; a progress from and through impersonation to identity. One might say that the "double
illusion" of Les Bonnes is a theatrical equivalent
to the frames of Genet's novels. The external
dimension of illusion is present in the conventional dramatic situation of actors disguised as
characters, of the "real" situation of those characters as maids in the service of Madame. The
inner dimension of illusion is composed of the
fantastical impersonations of Claire and Solange.
Both frames of course combine to confront the
spectator with the total artifice which is the
play, and which may be said to correspond to that
"absolute present" discernible in Notre-Dame-des-
Fleurs. A series of ironic inversions, however,
causes a degree of confusion between the two illusions of Les Bonnes. Madame, for example, is
seen by some critics as a foolish, artificial
creature, for whom the smoking of a cigarette is
quite as important as the pursuance of her lover
to Guiana or Siberia:

> Monsieur n'est pas coupable mais
> s'il l'était, avec quelle joie
> j'accepterais de porter sa croix!
> D'étape en étape, de prison en prison,
> et jusqu'au bagne je le suivrais.

A pied s'il le faut. Jusqu'au
bagne Solange!₈ Que je fume!
Une cigarette![8]

Whatever one may think of Madame's sincerity, her
professions lose something of their force for
having been anticipated by Claire in her opening
impersonation. Following upon the tense, ceremonious tirades of hatred Claire delivers as Madame,
the "real" Madame's complacent charity towards
her maids causes her to seem a travesty of Claire's
performance. In pushing illusion to the point at
which, with Claire's semi-suicide, it attains to
a reality, Claire and Solange both conclude and
invert their secret ritual.

Though technically a one-act play, Les
Bonnes is punctuated by a variety of domestic
bells - alarm-clocks, telephones, doorbells and a
klaxon - which divide it into five movements, reminiscent of a classical tragedy or comedy. The
play seems further to propound a tragic notion of
self-realisation; Claire and Solange find themselves committed to a course of action which, mag-
nificently, can only terminate with their destruc-
tion.[9] In another sense, however, Les Bonnes may
be termed surrealistic in its objectification of
oneiric states of mind.

In his third play, Le Balcon, Genet re-
linquishes his economical mode of construction
while retaining the illusionism of Les Bonnes.[10]
Le Balcon is set in a brothel, Mme Irma's "Le Grand
Balcon," an establishment known far and wide for
the peculiar nature of its services, and referred
to with both euphemism and literality as a House
of Illusions. The play is composed of nine tableaux and, according to the sense and scene of
action, may be further sub-divided into three parts.
As in Les Bonnes, the curtain rises on a twofold
imposture: in the first three tableaux, the audience behold successively a Bishop, Judge and General
engaged in stereotypical activities. It becomes
apparent, from odd lapses in the dialogue and
brusque interventions by Mme Irma, that these are

"in fact" ordinary mortals who pay substantial
sums of money for the privilege of acting out
their private, grand delusions in the sumptuous
décors of the brothel. It further transpires
that on this particular occasion a rebellion is
raging in the streets outside. In Mme Irma's
words, the revolutionaries seem undecided as to
whether their object is the Palais Royal or the
Grand Balcon. Opposing them is the Chief of
Police, a "real" dignitary and Irma's former
lover. In a long central tableau the Chief of
Police expresses anxiety that no client has yet
wished to impersonate him; his function having
apparently not yet captured the popular imagination, he feels insecure. In the ensuing section
of the play Chantal, a former prostitute, is
shown rehabilitated by the love of the leading
revolutionary, Roger the plumber. In the midst
of their idyll, Chantal is summoned to the barricades to sing and bring fervour to the partisans.
In the subsequent, concluding scenes, it appears
that the "real" figureheads of state - Bishop,
Judge, General and Queen - have been either killed,
rendered mad or reported missing; an envoy from
the battered palais Royal cynically invites the
imposters of the brothel to replace them which,
with some misgiving, they agree to do. The Queen,
who oddly and simply "is not," is replaced by
Mme Irma, thereby completing the parallel between
the Balcon and the Palace. Order is restored,
and the rebellion quashed. The move from fantasy
to reality does not, however, satisfy the preten-
ders, who are thus deprived of their capacity to
dream. Nor does her "real" role as latter-day
"Marseillaise" bring fortune to Chantal, for she
is assassinated at the precise instant of being
presented to the now royal Irma on the balcony.
In the final tableau, the defeated Roger pays his
first visit to the brothel and requests the décor -
a Leninesque mausoleum - prepared for the Chief of
Police. At first contented by his fantasy, Roger
proves reluctant to leave and return to reality.
He therefore performs a revolutionary act entirely
appropriate to the setting: he castrates himself.
Whereupon the actual Chief of Police feels free to

descend into his mausoleum for two millenia, intact
and secure in the new perdurability of his public
image. The play closes with Irma's address to
the audience: returning home they will, she assures
them, find matters to be even more illusory than in
the spectacle enacted.

As in <u>Les Bonnes</u>, therefore, the "double
frame" obtains; as in <u>Les Bonnes</u>, the "illusory"
content of the two frames is inverted. Most of
the characters, in their motion from the fantastic
to the real, meet with dissatisfaction or destruc-
tion; Roger, who moves in an inverse direction,
scarcely fares better. Only the cynical Envoy and
the Chief of Police remain unscathed. Despite the
evident illusions and inversions, however, critics
usually relate <u>Le Balcon</u> to the novel in which
Genet's characteristic double frame is least apparent: <u>Querelle de Brest</u>. The brothel of that
book, La Féria, is seen as a prototype for Le Grand
Balcon, Mme Lysiane as a forerunner of Irma, while
Lysiane's husband Norbert and the inspector Mario
are thought to be fused and reincarnate in the
Chief of Police.

Because of the caricatural presentation
of its social figureheads, the political qualifi-
cations of <u>Le Balcon</u> have not unnaturally been ex-
plored by critics. The same may be said of Genet's
fourth play, <u>Les Nègres</u>, itself a complex concatenation of ritual re-enactment of a crime, ritual
judgement and ritual execution. Once again, the
dual illusion is maintained from the outset. The
text specifically calls for black actors, half of
whom must wear grotesque white masks representing
the Governor, Lawyer, Valet, Missionary and Queen
of some archetypal colonial society; these figures
constitute the Court. They correspond to the General, Judge, Envoy, Bishop and Queen of <u>Le Balcon</u>,
and also recall, curiously, the executioner, lawyer,
judge and chaplain who enter Harcamone in <u>Miracle
de la Rose</u>. The unmasked blacks - Bobo, Neige,
Félicité, Vertu, Village, Diouf, Archibald and
Ville de Saint-Nazaire - must re-enact the rape
and murder of a youngish white woman. Which grisly

ritual is ostensibly to entertain the Court - the
designation being both legal and regal - and justify them in their bad opinion of the blacks. Significant in the re-enactment are Village, who apparently did the deed, Félicité, whose rôle is
analogous to that of the white Queen, and Archibald,
who controls the ritual with unflinching severity,
periodically reminding Village that he is not free
to indulge in any "white" sentimentality. At one
or two junctures the "white" court drop their masks,
uncovering themselves as blacks whom their play-
acting brothers applaud on their performance. The
ritual revolves around the draped coffin which supposedly contains the body of the murdered woman;
but when it is revealed that the catafalque is
empty, that the deed was never done, the Court
grasps with unease that its judicial power has
been symbolically eroded. After which realisation
the five personifications of an effete and deca-
dent colonialism are condemned to death and suffer
a simulated execution. Weaving in and out of this
action Ville de Saint-Nazaire, the one black who
is not clad in impeccable evening dress, reports
on the "real" offstage execution of a black inform-
er who has betrayed an imminent black revolt. The
ceremony devised for the white court is thus revealed as a distraction in both senses of the word,
intended to conceal the blacks' real activities;
yet since the Court is manifestly black, the disquieting conclusion to be drawn is that the ritual
is intended to distract the real, paying audience
from acts of black revolt. Since the play is pre-
faced by specific instructions that at least one
spectator be as white as possible, it would seem
that Genet means to explode his dual illusions with
a maximum of shock. In thus carrying a stage further the spectatorial involvement anticipated in
the final speech of Le Balcon, Genet is employing
the technique known ungrammatically as "total audience control."[11]

     With Les Nègres Genet seems to return to
the continuous dramatic form of Haute Surveillance
- punctuated, of course, by the various peripeteia
of the interchange 'twixt black and white. Some

critics, siding with the play's director, Roger
Blin, have also stressed the cyclic implications
of the ritual: when in conclusion the blacks
leave the stage dancing to Mozart, the minuet
which succeeds the pounding African rhythms is
deemed indicative of their future decadence. As
slaves, the blacks are strong; as conquerors, they
too will become effete and overcivilised, and so
decline.[12] This implicit cycle parallels to some
extent the form of the play's illusionism. The
white catafalque brought back on stage at the end
suggests that the sinister rite is liable to re-
commence. By this time the audience, doubly "dis-
illusioned," is in a position to apprehend the
disquieting corollary of their own participation.

In Les Paravents there re-appears the
form of disconnected tableaux employed in Le
Balcon. This fifth play, Genet's longest and,
some say, his greatest, casts more than ninety
characters and is again "political" in theme,
being set in Algeria at the time of a revolt.
This temporal particular itself, however, is something of an illusion, given Genet's penchant for
anachronism:

> Je n'ai pas le temps de vous
> en dire plus long pour vous faire
> comprendre que les soldats morts ou
> mourants dans cette pièce doivent
> avoir l'uniforme des soldats du duc
> d'Aumale et de Bugeaud. Le même
> mouvement du temps qui les dépose
> en Algérie les rejette à la mer.
> Même si, par leurs répliques, on
> comprend qu'ils vivaient en 1958.
> Cela n'a pas d'importance. Ils ont
> été imprudents.[13]

The mammoth cast falls naturally into groups: the
hero Saïd, his mother and his ugly wife; the people
of their village, including splendid hieratic prostitutes; the colonials - Sir Harold, the Blanken-
sees, the Vamp and their ilk; the French Army; and
the Arabs in revolt. The plot, if so it may be

termed, traces Saïd's determined fall through
shame towards incorrigible negation.[14] The poor-
est young man in his district, Said can afford
only the ugliest of wives, Leila, a girl so repulsive that she is obliged to wear a sack on her
head; Said continues to frequent the local brothel.
Wishing to cross the sea in search of better
things, Said steals the money for his fare. There
ensues the first of numerous spells in prison.
While Said pursues his heroic quest for ignominy,
his compatriots revolt; the colonial forces suffer
a series of humiliating, indeed fatal, reverses.
At this point the titular screens - themselves the
major elements of décor - assume a rôle in narrative. In Roger Blin's production, the actors play-
ing Arabs use the screens to make real, lurid
drawings of the triumphal atrocities perpetrated
on colonials. The screens further provide a
literal, if flimsy, barrier between the living
and the dead. After varying periods spent in the
limbo between the two states, most of the characters - the defeated French soldiers, Said's wife
and mother, the villagers, the prostitutes and
others who have died - burst through the paper
frames and are pleasantly amazed to find themselves in the harmonious, convivial society of the
deceased. Only Saïd refuses to be named among the
dead or the living, but pursues his solitary tra-
jectory towards a legendary negation.

        Although Les Paravents contains no double
frame, no play within a play, the actual screens
constitute an objectification of illusion itself.
Embellished with depictions of the violent deeds,
the screens are at once real, theatrical objects
and an instrument of narrative; if re-enacted, the
said deeds would technically belong to the "inner
frame." In another sense, the screens may be said
to resolve the endless re-reflections - themselves
emphasised literally in Le Balcon by Irma's numerous,
sumptuous mirrors - of preceding plays. In bursting
through these flimsy delimitations of mortality the
actors do, after all, abolish a barrier analagous
to the reflective surface of a mirror.[15] Les Paravents thus constitute a satisfying resolution of

140

dialectical reflection; it is, however, in Genet's
middle play, <u>Le Balcon</u>, that the comic properties
of re-reflection would seem best exemplified.

(b) The Part of Parody: <u>Le Balcon</u>

        The humorous elements of Genet's theatre
first become noticeable in <u>Les Bonnes</u>. Even if
<u>Haute Surveillance</u> is considered a parody of Jan-
senistic metaphysics, as Philip Thody has suggested,
its general tone does not encourage mirth. The
double illusions of Genet's second drama do, however, permit of a parodical interpretation that is
partly comic. Accept the Sartrian contention that
Genet intended the roles to be played by boys, and
<u>Les Bonnes</u> may be deemed a travesty in both a
literal and a comic sense. The presentation of
Madame, too, involves a form of double parody, contingent upon the rather flat impression created by
Madame at her own real entrance. As readily appears
from their respective remarks, Madame's insipid ex-
clamations - "De plus en plus! Des glaïeuls hor-
ribles, d'un rose débilitant, et du mimosa! Ces
folles doivent courir les halles avant le jour pour
les acheter moins cher. Tant de sollicitude, ma
chère Solange..." - are feeble in comparison with
the initial diatribe of Claire as Madame:

                CLAIRE (debout, en combinaison,
                tournant le dos à la coiffeuse.
                Son geste - le bras tendu - et le
                ton, seront d'un tragique exaspéré).

                    Et ces gants! Ces éternels gants!
                Je t'ai dit assez souvent de les
                laisser à la cuisine. C'est avec ça,
                sans doute, que tu espères séduire le
                laitier. Non, non, ne mens pas, c'est
                inutile. Pends-les au-dessus de
                l'évier. Quand comprendras-tu que
                cette chambre ne doit pas être
                souillée?[16]

Claire's witticism is doubly potent. The rubber

kitchen gloves in question, possibly suggestive
of a cow's udders, both emphasise and undercut
whatever gentility Solange might hope to manifest
by wearing gloves. Madame's effusions betray only
an ironic ignorance as to her servants' actual
feelings. Both Claire and her employer - Claire
with her vitriol and her Racinian stance, Madame
with her complacent silliness - seem to travesty
a quintessential Madameness. A comparable form
of parody, a product both of stereotype and situation, will constitute the principal comic resource
of Genet's next play, Le Balcon.

      The author's generally disgruntled re-
actions - expressed in Comment jouer le Balcon -
to early productions of this work terminate upon
the clear instruction:

> Encore une chose: ne pas jouer
> cette pièce comme si elle était une
> satire de ceci ou cela. Elle est,
> - elle sera donc jouée comme - la
> glorification de l'Image et du Reflet.
> Sa signification - satirique ou non -
> apparaitra seulement dans ce cas.[17]

In other words, satirical components in this work
can only become properly apparent if the text is
treated with ceremonious respect. This paradox
was appreciated by the British critic of the
Listener who objected to a BBC Third Programme
performance on the grounds that its misguided
use of "comic" suburban accents completely deflated
the imposing aspects of the protagonists' impersonations:

> To get Genet's genuine humour across,
> you have to avoid the wrong sort of
> laughs - a difficult job, as his own
> touch is so erratic...After all it's
> part of Genet's point that you should
> feel the performances put on in the
> brothel are not far from the real thing;
> the clients and their fantasies should
> be formidable as well as comic.[18]

Though it supports our contention that humour does exist in Genet's universe, albeit in eccentric form, Mr Furbank's remark about "erratic" touch does present analogies with several pejorative judgements on Le Balcon. Richard Coe, for example, points to uncertainties of objective and technique which render it the least satisfactory of Genet's plays. Comparing Le Balcon unfavourably with Les Nègres, Mr Coe observes:

> In The Blacks, the dialectic at bottom is just as complex as in The Balcony, but its complexity is hidden and is only revealed by implication. In The Balcony, every step in the dialectic is argued out stage by stage between the characters, and the result is as though Brecht and Gabriel Marcel had taken a hand at writing scenes in the same production: an unevenness, a lack of balance which destroys precisely that element to which Genet attaches most importance - the absolute belief which the audience should accord to the symbolic dramatic figures who dominate the action.[19]

For analytical, rather than evaluative purposes, however, this technical imbalance may actually prove advantageous, the evident dialectical bias providing a convenient framework for disquisition.

In Le Balcon parody is not, as was largely the case in the Biblical portions of Notre-Dame-des-Fleurs, an oddly solemn product of literary burlesque; rather it is a product of dramatic situation. In confronting his audience with the apparent spectacle of a Bishop indulging in grandiloquence within a brothel, Genet obliges the spectator, by implication, to recall the habitual functions of such establishments as well as the habitual functions of a prelate. This circumstance resembles literary parody inasmuch as it involves a comic superimposition which both travesties and recalls the original model. In addition, the actual term "House of Illusions" ironically implies erotic de-

lusion on the part of patrons of the usual type
of brothel. To the spectator's initial amusement
at finding social pillars in that place may be
added his amusement at finding plumbers and their
ilk masquerading as Bishop, Judge and General,
this latter circumstance being an inversion of
the former. This double comedy is at all times
dependent on illusion, first established, then
destroyed, but always contained within the absolute theatrical illusion of performance.

The first tableau brings to dramatic
culmination Genet's enduring proclivity for combining the sacred and profane. The erotic component in the combination is discreetly indicated
in stage directions:

> Le décor semble représenter une
> sacristie, formée de trois paravents
> de satin, rouge sang.
> Dans le paravent du fond une porte
> est ménagée.
> Au-dessus un énorme crucifix
> espagnol, dessiné en trompe-l'oeil.
> Sur la paroi de droite un miror -
> dont le cadre est doré et sculpté -
> reflète un lit défait qui, si la piéce
> était disposée logiquement, se trouve-
> rait dans la salle, aux premiers fau-
> teuils de l'orchestre.
> (Balcon, p. 11)

The objects designated are, in Genet's universe,
familiar, significant and - for patrons of the
stalls - somewhat disconcerting. If screens anticipate the décors of Les Paravents, mirror and
chandelier recall those of 'Adame Miroir, while
the trompe-l'oeil crucifix is reminiscent of characteristic devices of Notre-Dame-des-Fleurs; the
unmade bed, however, being theoretically situated
in the front row of the stalls serves as a reminder
of the house's primary function and implies that
spectators from select regions of the auditorium
are indeed in the brothel. The "Bishop" is presented as a Bishop, that is, not as an impersonator -

"...L'Evêque, mitré et chapeau doré, est assis
dans le fauteuil." Yet stage directions specify
that the actor be on stilts eighteen inches high -
"Il est manifestement plus grand que nature" -
once again implying both caricature and aggrandise-
ment.

Dialogue in this opening tableau simultaneously evokes and contrasts in humorous wise
the two functions of "Le Grand Balcon." As in the
two succeeding scenes, the principal comic resorts
are interruption and juxtaposition of inapposite
tones. Thus Irma's blunt financial reminders in-
trude repeatedly upon her client's lofty reveries.
With the insidious amiability of a lower middle-
class French shopkeeper - and rather as one might
imagine a Madame eliciting descriptions of positions and perversions used - she solicits an account of the fake Bishop's performance: "(Soudain
aimable, insidieuse) Et qu'est-ce que nous avons
accompli ce soir? Bénédiction? Prière? Messe?
Adoration perpétuelle?" (Balcon, p. 14) On learn-
ing that the client has conducted a Blessing and
Confession, Irma becomes professionally concerned
and presses for more detail: "Vous permettez que
je m'inquiète...professionellement? Je vous ai
dit deux mille." (Balcon, p. 15) Exasperated by
such interruptions, the Bishop eventually dismisses
the two women and endeavours to conclude his perora-
tion on the symbols of office:

> ...Mitres, dentelles, tissus d'or
> et de verroteries, génuflexions...
> Aux chiottes la fonction!
> > > (Crépitement de mitrail-
> > > leuse)
> > IRMA (passant la tête par la
> > porte entre-baillée)
> Vous avez fini?
> > L'EVEQUE
>
> Mais laissez-moi, nom de Dieu. Foutez
> le camp! Je m'interroge.
> > > (Balcon, p. 22)

His meditations are again comically abbreviated,
however, by Irma and the girl who ultimately man-
ages to disrobe him; the spectacle of prostitute
and Madame defrocking false prelate is attended
by the slightly vulgar implications of the client's
not having finished. To these comic factors may
be added the extreme disorder of the situation,
the scene being additionally punctuated by screams
emanating from a neighbouring room, and by volleys
of machine-gun fire heard ricocheting in the
street outside.

The intended theme of Le Balcon - the
glorification of the Image and its Reflection -
finds objective manifestation in the presence of
mirrors as indicated in stage directions for the
first four tableaux. Erotic and oneiric functions
are also delegated to Mme Irma's girls, upon whose
histrionic talent depends the clients' satisfaction. Essential to that satisfaction is a wholly
desirable reflection of the client's self as depicted in the act of fantasy. Should for any
reason that reflection be less than satisfactory,
a psychological difficulty develops not unlike
the one facing characters in Sartre's Huis-Clos:
a perpetually frustrated imperative that the esti-
mation of others coincide with the individual's
perception of the self. The actresses' performances are, again, double. As Irma's favourite em-
ployee Carmen makes clear in the disproportionately
long fifth tableau, the oneiric satisfaction of
the client also constitutes the oneiric satisfaction of the girl; the performances of hostess and
dreamer are interdependent. Carmen, for example,
was a gifted and contented Immaculate Conception
before being promoted to the spiritually unsatisfy-
ing post of cashier. In the opening tableau, it
is the mirror, rather than the girl, which reflects
the Bishop's Image: "Répondez donc, miroir.
Répondez-moi. Est-ce que je viens ici découvrir
le mal et l'innocence? Et dans vos glaces dorées,
qu'étais-je?" (Balcon, p. 21) The girl does contribute to the comic of the situation in that doubt
over the veracity of her six confessed sins frus-
trates the Bishop and justifies a comic juxtaposi-

tion of fantastic and prosaic tones:

> IRMA
> Dans ses beaux yeux, monseigneur,
> le repentir, au moins est-il passé?

> L'EVEQUE (se levant)
> Au galop. Mais, est-ce que j'y
> cherchais le repentir? J'y vis le
> désir gourmand de la faute.
> (<u>Balcon</u>, p. 18)

In the second and third <u>tableaux</u>, the reflective
aspects of the oneiric function are almost wholly
concentrated in the girls, themselves variously
assisted by Pimp Arthur in disguise. As in the
preceding scene, comic effect is generated by constant shifts in tone, and by the client's frustration in failing to project and perceive a wholly
appropriate Image of the self. As the second scene
commences, the aspiring Judge is viewed crawling
towards a prostitute cast as shoplifter; rapidly,
however, his ridiculous humility is replaced by
severity as he attempts to force a confession;
later, domination once again gives way to a posture
of abjection as he implores the girl to confess.
Since the girl is new, and since it is hard to
ensure a psychologically satisfying sequence in
enacted fantasy, frustration is caused by premature
avowal:

> LE JUGE (très doux,
>   implorant)
> ...Dis-moi, mon petit, je t'en
> supplie, dis-moi que tu es une voleuse.

> LA VOLEUSE
> Oui, monsieur le juge!

> LE BOURREAU
> Non!

> LA VOLEUSE (le regardant,
>   étonnée)
> Non!

LE BOURREAU

C'est pour plus tard...Je dis, l'aveu
doit venir en son heure.

(Balcon, pp. 28-9)

Genet's procedure at this point is doubly ironic.
For one thing, the spectacle of Judge pleading with
his victim constitutes a startling, if crude, reversal of judicial processes; for another, the
misplaced confession nullifies the preceding dialogue. At the culmination of the scene, a yet more
damning reversal is inflicted on the Judge. According to the logic of his own fantasy - implacable in
the rigour of its re-reflections - his position as
a judge is dependent on confession, if the girl
refuses to confess, she cannot, to the judge's satisfaction, be judged as a thief; if thieves do not
exist, there can be no judges either:

LE JUGE

Mademoiselle...Madame. Je vous
en prie. (Il se jette à genoux.)
Voyez, je vous en supplie? Ne me
laissez pas dans une pareille posture,
attendant d'être juge? S'il n'y avait
pas de juge, où irions-nous, mais s'il
n'y avait pas de voleurs?

LA VOLEUSE (ironique)

Et s'il n'y en avait pas?

LE JUGE

Ce serait terrible. Mais vous
ne me jouerez pas un tour pareil, n'est-
ce pas? Vous ne ferez pas qu'il n'y en
ait pas?

(Balcon, p. 39)

Exchanges such as this bear out Genet's contention
that whatever satire is contained in the play can
only become properly observable through a solemn
glorification of the Image and its Reflection.
According to the Judge's logic the social order,

as represented by himself, would without miscreants
cease to exist. If the implications of Reflection
are carried to their logical extreme, the audience
too becomes a target of satire. In situating a reflected rumpled bed right in the stalls, Genet's
stage directions imply the spectator's presence in
the brothel. Carried thus into the auditorium, the
Reflection would seem to pre-suppose an audience
composed of prelates, barristers and other reactionary variations on the Sartrian Just Man. While,
therefore, it is demonstrable that satire in Le
Balcon is indeed dependent on the dialectic of
Reflection, it may also be objected that Genet is
guilty of a certain ideological simplification; his
audiences, after all, tend also to contain left-
wing intellectuals.[20]

In the third tableau the erotic function
of brothels - the inter-sexual act - is parodied
more appreciably than in the two preceding scenes
by a sort of circumstantial pun on connotations of
the verb "to mount." The timid general's projected
self-image requires as its reflective complement
not brother officers or the defeated foe but his
faithful horse, Colombe, as played by another one
of Irma's virtuosic girls. After a preparatory
conversation comically punctuated by cries from
the adjoining room, Irma's departure permits the
farcical exchange:

LE GENERAL

...Et tu es en retard, qu'est-ce que
tu foutais? On ne t'avait pas donné
ton sac d'avoine? Tu souris? Tu
souris à ton cavalier? Tu reconnais
sa main, douce et ferme? (Il la flatte.)
Mon fier coursier! Ma belle jument,
avec toi nous en avons gagné des galops!

LA FILLE

Et ce n'est pas fini! Mes sabots
bien ferrés, de mes pattes nerveuses je
veux arpenter le monde. Retirez votre
pantalon et vos souliers, que je vous
habille.   (Balcon, p. 48)

Noticeably more articulate than the preceding girls,
"Colombe" is charged not with the General's physical person - though she does at one point kneel
before him like a circus horse - but with the task
of reflecting his military dignity, of giving utterance to the lyrical essence of his victory and
death. Throughout her somewhat stereotypical depiction of battle and demise, however, "Colombe"
retains her metaphorical identity as mount:

LA FILLE

...Au détour d'une rue, un linge bleu
m'effraya: Je me cabrai, mais domptée
par ta douce et lourde main, mon tremble-
ment cessa. Je repris l'amble. Comme
je t'aimais, mon héros!

LE GENERAL

Mais...les morts? N'y avait-il
pas de morts?

Reflecting Genet's lasting and not always reverent
fixation with funereal rites, the tableau concludes
with a sketchy parody of the obsequy typically
accorded national heroes: the General's "corpse"
sprawled upon a chair, "Colombe" makes equine stepping motions while intoning the Funeral March from
Chopin's second sonata. Initially a travesty of
sexual coupling, "Colombe's" metaphorical incarna-
tion further evokes the riderless horse characteristic of state funerals. As so frequently occurs in
Genet's works, the parody involves a duplication:
stage directions prefacing the scene require a
small model horse, "...un cheval dont se servent
les danseurs folkloriques avec une petite jupe
plissée." (Balcon, p. 42)   This tiny steed is
symbolically lifted over "Colombe's" head by her
spurious master just before the commencement of
the funeral procession. In its aspect of self-
parody - the ludicrous re-duplication of an act -
the gesture is reminiscent of Divine's two heroic
auto-coronations in Notre-Dame-des-Fleurs. It is
a curious footnote to this termination that "Colombe"
- the name itself is ridiculous for a military

horse - is at this point referred to by the General
as "mon beau genêt d'Espagne," a phrase applied by
Genet to himself on more than one occasion.[21] Assuming it is not mere verbal accident, this nominal
coincidence does imply a faintly startling development in the relationship of audience to author.

It would appear, from the three opening
scenes of Le Balcon, that the play's major source
of comedy derives from the double parody of certain
functions, stereotypical within the context of the
drama, explicitly social and implicitly erotic.
In the extensive, minutely argued fifth tableau,
additional such situations are no longer enacted
but are enumerated a trifle sardonically by Carmen
as she describes the emotional perils of performance:

CARMEN

...Vous observez tout ça de loin,
patronne, mais si une seule fois
vous mettiez la robe et le voile
bleu, ou si vous étiez la pénitente
dégrafée, ou la jument du général,
ou la paysanne culbutée dans la
paille...

IRMA (choquée)

Ou la soubrette en tablier rose, ou
l'archiduchesse dépucelée par le
gendarme ou... enfin, je ne vais pas
vous énumérer la nomenclature, vous
sauriez ce que cela laisse dans l'âme,
et qu'il faut bien qu'on s'en défasse
avec un peu d'ironie.
(Balcon, p. 63)

Carmen's plaint being precisely that Mme Irma,
financially alert and ever-conscious of professional
decorum will not permit the girls the luxury of
laughter, it becomes clear that the solemnity which
should attend presentation of the play must also
obtain in the inner frame of illusion created in

the brothel. As Irma herself concedes, "Un éclat
de rire, ou même un sourire fout tout par terre.
S'il y a sourire, il y a doute." (Balcon, p. 63)
What most interestingly emerges from Irma and
Carmen's decortication of their clients' proclivi-
ties, however, is the relationship discernible between parody and Genet's cherished device of the
trompe-l'oeil. It transpires that in almost every
instance of Irma's commercial illusionism a client
requests essential details, "true" and "false,"
which both undercut and enhance the artful semblance. Thus, embellishing upon the presentation
of Sainte-Thérèse which she proposes as a distraction for her bored favourite Carmen, Irma reveals
that the authentic detail will be a wedding-ring -
"c'est à cela qu'il saura qu'il a affaire à une
vraie religieuse" - while the spurious particular
will consist of black lace underwear beneath the
nun's habit. Since such particulars emphasise
both the "real" and the "fake," Sainte-Thérèse's
frilly knickers are in a sense analogous to the
artificial spot on the face of a great beauty.
Though not precisely similar, inclusion of the inauthentic detail, especially, does bear comparison
with the trompe-l'oeil, itself habitually defined
as a visual deception in which objects are rendered
in minute detail, emphasising the illusion of
tactile and spatial qualities. In its painstaking
mimesis of an agreed reality, the skillful trompe-
l'oeil thus appears almost to coincide with its
original model; yet, paradoxically, the degree to
which it succeeds must necessarily be measured by
some minor flaw. Were it not for that slight imperfection, the imitation would risk coinciding
with reality, since perfect mimesis is of necessity
reality itself. Like the artist whose work must
by definition avoid this total coincidence in order
to be art, Irma's clients and girls depend upon
the inauthentic detail, the spurious particular
becomes the measure of Irma's commercial illusionism. This is apparent in the sequence in which
Arthur, supposedly engaged to "play" at being dead
for the delectation of a Cabinet official, is hit
by a stray bullet and transformed into a corpse.
Thus, in the seventh tableau, to the Envoy's de-

lighted exclamation: "Ce corps l'eût fait se pâmer, notre cher ministre," Irma replies: "N'en croyez rien, monsieur l'Envoyé. Ce que veulent ces messieurs, c'est le trompe l'oeil. Le Ministre désirait un faux cadavre." (Balcon, p. 131) Thus, Irma's presentation of Sainte-Thérèse and the deceptive trompe-l'oeil both admit of comparison with parody in the extent to which all three measure their effect in terms of deviation from an accepted model.

The implicit and explicit travesties of certain characters and situations, stereotypical within the context of the play, constitute the principal parodical elements of the first half of Le Balcon. In later scenes, irony predominates - chiefly the ironic transformation of illusion into actuality, and back again. This systematic shuttle operates even in the sixth tableau, in exchanges between Chantal, Roger and the rebels - to all appearances those characters most solidly planted in the conventional reality of the outer dramatic frame. Chantal, the renegade prostitute who has been rehabilitated and returned to the outer world by her trusty lover Roger, exchanges with him such archetypal amorous professions that even he is led to ask: "Tu connais tous les rôles, n'est-ce pas? Tout à l'heure, tu me donnais la réplique?" (Balcon, p. 128) Since Chantal promptly returns to rôle-playing as symbolic songstress of the revolution, her contacts with wholesome reality are relatively short-lived. The ironic inversion of illusion which, in the play's seventh tableau, brings to a semblance of power and real exercise of function Irma, Bishop, General and Judge, constitutes a crushing inversion of reality for the rebels, who are then faced with an illusion they take to be real: that of four fresh figureheads. Similarly, their own acquisition of a symbol - Chantal - speeds their defeat. It is significant that the scene which shows Irma appearing publicly upon the balcony and recognised as Queen - the brief tableau VIII - is the scene of Chantal's death; like Arthur, she is shot through the head by a bullet presumed stray. Irma subsequently accuses the Bishop of assassination:

> IRMA
>
> ...(A l'Evèque.) Si vous n'aviez pas
> eu l'idée abominable de faire assassi-
> ner Chantal...
>
> L'EVEQUE (faussement apeuré)
>
> Balle perdue!
>
> IRMA
>
> Perdue ou non la balle, Chantal
> a été assassinée sur le Balcon, sur
> MON Balcon! Alors qu'elle revenait
> ici pour me voir, pour revoir sa
> patronne...
>
> L'EVEQUE
>
> J'ai eu la présence d'esprit
> d'en faire une de nos saintes.
>
> LE CHEF DE LA POLICE
>
> Attitude traditionnelle. Réflexe
> d'homme d'église...
> (Balcon, p. 173)

This exchange is heavily laced with dramatic
irony, since it indicates substantiation of Irma's
previously expressed fear that the rebels might
confuse the Palais Royal with her brothel. That
Le Grand Balcon does indeed become the royal house
implies, conversely, that the seat of government
is a seat of whoring. The Bishop's stratagem -
the canonisation of Chantal - typifies the cynical
manipulations of illusion and reality characteristic of the established order in the play's later
portions. Similarly, irony and satire inform the
scene in which the three young photographers, re-
sorting to such parodical expedients as the sub-
stitution of the Judge's monocle for the Blessed
Host, produce real images from faked events. The
two functions of the House of Illusions - the
erotic and the oneiric - parodied implicitly and

explicitly in the play's opening scenes are again
ironically conjoined in the ultimate tableau when
Roger, driven by defeat to fantastic indulgence as
Police Chief, reluctant to quit his Leninesque tomb,
commits the sacrilegious self-castration. Roger's
deed, which apparently bloodies carpets and appals
Mme Irma, symbolically fuses and destroys both the
sexual and the social order of Irma's Grand Balcon.

     The double theatrical illusion obtaining
in Le Balcon - obtaining, indeed, in four of Genet's
five published plays - may be said to correspond
to the double structure characteristic of his novels
and even of his first two poems. Just as artistic
composition emerges as the subject of Marche funèbre,
of Notre-Dame-des-Fleurs, the conscious use of artifice within a frame of theatrical convention is
both a theme and a major dramatic mechanism of the
plays. In Le Balcon, as in the early poems and
novels, interaction between the two frames is effected by inversion. In Notre-Dame-des-Fleurs, an
incarcerated narrator paradoxically asserts his
freedom by dooming the creatures of his inner frame,
thereby inverting his own situation; the author of
Le Balcon is constantly inverting an inter-dependent
reality and illusion, an inversion which generates
and is generated by elements parodical and ironic.
Like most of Genet's works, Le Balcon is permeated
by the theme of song; the workings of which theme
are themselves connected to the workings of irony.

(c) Song and Dance

     The theme of "song" in Le Balcon is most
noticeably incarnate in Irma's two most talented
performers, Carmen and Chantal, both of whose names
derive from Latin words connoting melodic utterance;
carmen has retained both its Latin form and meanings
of "song," "poem" or "incantation," while "Chantal"
is a Gallic derivative of the verbal form cantare.
Despite this nominal resemblance, the two ladies
are reflectively opposed in their dramatic functions. Like "Colombe," the girl who has the task

of putting into lyrical pronouncement the quintessentials of the General's fantasy, Carmen is a
gifted performer whose interpretation of the Immaculate Conception metaphorically elicits song
from a teller of the Credit Lyonnais:

> Devant la Madone que j'étais, un
> Espagnol aurait pu prier et former
> des serments. Il me chantait, me
> confondant avec la couleur qu'il
> chérissait, et quand il m'emportait
> sur le lit, c'est dans le bleu qu'il
> pénétrait.
>
> (Balcon, pp. 80-1)

The "song" which she calls forth being an indica-
tion of her virtuosity, Carmen might be termed
the lyrical inspiration of the inner framework of
illusion. In this she opposes Chantal, who leaves
the brothel for the world, supposedly preferring
illusion to reality. A recidivist of rôle-playing,
however, Chantal, not Carmen, becomes the figure-
head of whom Irma ironically inquires: "Dans
toute révolution, il y a la putain exaltée qui
chante une Marseillaise et se virginise. Tu
seras celle-là?" (Balcon, p. 83) As a symbolic
songstress of revolt, Chantal ostensibly becomes
the inspiration of the outer frame, of that domain
in which characters are what they appear to be, and
not double actors. Yet the prudish, chaste, determined rebels are paradoxically weakened by their
symbol, just as the Chief of Police predicts:

IRMA

Roger...fait partie du réseau
Andromède.

LE CHEF DE LA POLICE

Andromède? Bravo. La révolte
s'exalte et s'exile d'ici-bas. Si
elle donne à ses secteurs des noms de
constellation, elle va vite s'évaporer
et se métamorphoser en chants.
Souhaitons-les beaux.

156

> IRMA
>
> Et si leurs chants donnent aux
> révoltés du courage? Et qu'ils
> veuillent mourir pour eux?
>
> LE CHEF DE LA POLICE
>
> La beauté de leurs chants les
> amollira. Malheureusement, ils n'en
> sont pas à ce stade, ni de la beauté,
> ni di la mollesse. En tous les cas les
> amours de Chantal furent providentielles.
> (<u>Balcon</u>, pp. 109-10)

Multiple ironies thus attend Chantal's revolutionary
exaltation. First, as we have seen, her excursion
into external reality ends in play-acting; second,
the symbol she becomes is self-defeating; third, the
aspiration which was to have caused a victorious
Chantal to sing from the balcony ends in her death.
As envisioned by the rebel in <u>tableau</u> VI, Chantal
leads the attack: "A l'aube, comme tu le sais,
nous attaquons le Palais. Chantal entrera la
première, d'un balcon elle chantera. C'est tout."
(<u>Balcon</u>, p. 122) When Chantal does confront a
regal Irma on the balcony, the latter curtsies,
implying either irony or a recognition of superiority; in the same instant Chantal, struck by a
bullet, falls at her feet. For Chantal, therefore, the interplay of illusion and reality is
mortally resolved on the balcony of the House of
Illusions, on that external protrusion of the house
from which the established order presents its
ridiculously aggrandised Image to the world, on the
balcony from which she had been meant to sing. Her
demise partly parallels that of Arthur who, at the
end of his incongruous quest for the Chief of Police, is smitten by a bullet just as he recounts
the furies of the crowd:

> J'ai réussi à atteindre le Palais-
> Royal, et j'ai vu le Grand Chambellan
> ... Et je suis reparti. Les femmes
> sont les plus exaltées. Elles en-
> couragent au pillage et à la tuerie.

> Mais la plus terrible, c'est une
> fille qui chantait...
>
> (On entend un claquement sec.
> Une vitre de la fenêtre vole en
> éclats. Un miroir aussi, près du
> lit.
> Arthur tombe, frappé au front,
> d'une balle venue du dehors...)
> (Balcon, p. 115)

The two deaths differ, clearly, in that Arthur,
having momentarily evoked a fragment of external
reality, expires within the world of illusion,
felled by a bullet from outside; Chantal, having
brought illusion to the outer world, is felled at
the General's behest by a bullet from the ranks
of an illusory establishment. Memory of revolutionary song attends Arthur's death; Chantal
dies at the instant she was supposed to have sung.
The notion of song, therefore - an implacable,
superior and lyrical species of reality - is
intimately linked with the ironic interaction of
the inner and the outer frames.

Le Balcon is typical of Genet's later
plays in that it contains the theme of festivity;
as Carmen remarks to Irma, "Votre maison a pour
elle d'apporter la consolation. Vous montez et
préparez leurs théâtres clandestins." (Balcon,
p. 75) And, as Irma replies slightly later in
that scene, "Ici, la Comédie, l'Apparence se
gardent pures, la Fête intacte." (Balcon, p. 76)
Or, as Carmen again observes: "Autour de votre
belle personne vous avez pu organiser un théâtre
fastueux, une fête dont les splendeurs vous en-
veloppent, vous dissimulant au monde." (Balcon,
p. 80)[22] The theme of festivity, coupled with
the concept of the secret rite, will pervade both
Les Nègres and Les Paravents. At the climax of
her long invocation: "Dahomey! ... Dahomey! ...
A mon secours, Nègres," Félicité, the black anti-
queen of Les Nègres, issues a global invitation
to the clandestine performance:

158

> Afrique boudeuse, Afrique travaillée
> dans le feu, dans le fer, Afrique
> aux millions d'esclaves royaux, Afrique
> déportée, continent à la dérive, tu es
> là? Lentement vous vous évanouissez,
> vous reculez dans le passé, les récits
> de naufrages, les musées coloniaux, les
> travaux des savants, mais je vous
> rappelle ce soir pour assister à une
> fête secrète.[23]

At the beginning of his Lettres à Roger Blin - a
series of instructions written privately to the
director of Les Paravents, and subsequently published - Genet insists upon the importance of festivity:

> Je vous dis cela parce que la
> fête, si limitée dans le temps et
> l'espace, apparemment destinée à
> quelques spectateurs, sera d'une telle
> gravité qu'elle sera aussi destinée aux
> morts. Personne ne doit être écarté
> ou privé de la fête: il faut qu'elle
> soit si belle que les morts aussi la
> devinent, et qu'ils en rougissent.
> Si vous réalisez Les Paravents, vous
> devez aller toujours dans le sens de
> la fête unique, et très loin en elle.[24]

Themes of song and dance occur quite naturally in
accordance with festivity. In Les Nègres, where
the celebration is a solemn, secret and rebellious
rite, song is both literal and metaphorical. The
thighs of Village, for example, "sing" as he ad-
dresses the white woman - farcically played by
Diouf - whom he will rape and kill: "C'est un pays
lointain, mais que tout mon corps pourrait vous
réciter. Ecoutez chanter mes cuisses! Ecoutez!"
(Nègres, p. 91) Song is literally present in the
lyrical snatches chanted by Bobo, Village, Neige
and Vertu to the refrain of the Dies Irae:

> VILLAGE (chant sur l'air du
> "dies irae")

Madame...Madame...

> NEIGE (sur le "dies irae")
>
> Entrez, entrez... délivrez-nous du mal.
> Alléluiah.
>
>   BOBO (maintenant toutes les
>   répliques seront chantées
>   sur cet air)
>
> O descendez, mes cataractes!
>   (Nègres, p. 112)

Certain invocations of Les Nègres - most notably
Félicité's "Dahomey!" and its white equivalent,
pronounced by the Queen - attain to the solemnity
of ritual incantation. Appropriately, the theme
of song is accompanied in Les Nègres by that of
dance, in a form which particularly emphasises
the tension generated between the two represented
cultures:

> Quand le rideau est tiré,
> quatre nègres en frac... et quatre
> négresses en robe du soir dansent
> autour du catafalque une sorte de
> menuet sur un air de Mozart, qu'ils
> sifflent et fredonnent.
>   (Nègres, p. 15)

At the play's termination, the actors dance wildly
to an African pulsating beat; rebellious vigour
triumphs over mannered decadence. After a while,
however, the native rhythms are replaced by the
exquisite strains of Don Giovanni, thereby indicating that black potency will flourish, wither
and decay.[25]

In Genet's last published play, Les
Paravents, the theme of song dominates the work's
conclusion. As the final scene begins, Arab villagers and the now reconciled society of dead respectively await the arrival of Saïd, the unregen-
erate prodigal son whose quest for abjection is
drawing to its close. An ironic celebration
awaits Saïd: as Bachir puts it, "On voulait te
faire une fête. On la prépare. Ici et chez les

morts."[26] Saïd's reception is nonetheless problematical; for one thing, there is doubt as to what
to do with one who has fallen so far that the normal
social judgements are impossible. As Saïd rapidly
perceives, the festivity awaiting him is death:
"Vous allez me tuer d'abord, n'est-ce pas? Alors
faites-le tout de suite! Vous m'attendiez, c'est
ma fête..."(Paravents, p. 251) To Saïd's fury,
however, Ommou wishes him ambivalently dead: "...
c'est mort qu'on te veut mais c'est vivant pas
mort..."(Paravents, p. 251)   It is in response to
Saïd's enraged exclamation - "C'est me laisser
vivant pour mort!" - that Ommou introduces the
theme of song:

> Et s'il fallait chanter, chanter
> ... S'il fallait inventer Saïd... S'il
> fallait mot par mot, ici et la, cracher,
> baver toute une histoire... écrite ou
> récitée ... baver l'histoire Saïd...
> (Paravents, p. 252)

The guardian then provides the essential themes for
the song of Saïd: the loves of Saïd and Leila as
recounted by a man condemned to death:

> Un chant s'élève! J'ai appris
> à chanter comme eux, du mollet, du
> jarret, et même de l'intestin! (Tout
> le monde rit.) Quoi, vous rigolez?
> (Sévère) Vous n'avez jamais entendu
> chanter l'intestin des condamnés à
> mort? C'est que vous n'écoutez pas.
> (Noble, il annonce.) Les amours de
> Saïd et de Leila par l'intestin d'un
> condamné à mort.
> (Paravents, p. 253)

The progression of themes in this bizarre celebration is thus from moral decay - the glorious
"pourriture" of Saïd - to physical decay and death,
and thence to song. At this juncture, however, con-
testation occurs; a young soldier, a bawdy personi-
fication of Cartesian logic and patriotic principles, contests the value of such song: "Mais nous
on est vivant, je parle de ceux d'entre nous encore

vivants, dis-moi donc si la tête coupée des clebs doit nous apporter là-bas l'histoire de Saïd?" (Paravents, p. 253) In response, Ommou delivers herself of her most significant offhand pronouncement on the nature of the irrational and the indemonstrable:

> Soldat! ...Soldat de chez nous,
> jeune peau de con, il y a des vérités
> qui ne doivent jamais être appliquées.
> C'est celles-là qu'on doit faire vivre
> par le chant qu'elles sont devenues...
>
> Certaines vérités sont inapplicables
> sinon elles mourraient...Elles ne
> doivent pas mourir mais vivre par le
> chant qu'elles sont devenues... Vive
> le chant!
> (Paravents, p. 254)

One may assume that this response is important to Genet, for its contents recur, in almost identical terms, in preface to his recent essay on Rembrandt; furthermore, the Lettres à Roger Blin specifically advocate a casual delivery of these lines, since solemn emphasis would tend to destroy their point.[27] In the remainder of the scene, Saïd is summarily executed by the soldiers, but fails to appear in the domain of the deceased. The play thus closes on a question: "Où il est?" asks his mother; Kadidja replies, ambiguously, "Chez les morts." (Paravents, p. 260)

Curiously, Genet's translator Bernard Frechtman has altered the play's last line, making it a double question posed by Saïd's mother: "Then where is he? In a song?"[28] This alteration clearly reflects the mood of the scene, but betrays the ambivalence of Genet's termination. If Kadidja, who is herself "dead," thus herself "chez les morts," can pronounce Saïd "with the dead," where he is manifestly not, a possible implication is that no-one, except Leila and Saïd, is really dead in Les Paravents; the whole theatrical illusion of the screens would thus be destroyed. The result

is the same: nothing remains but memory of the
song which, as in <u>Le Balcon</u>, becomes a superior,
inapplicable form of verity endowed with mortal
import. Saïd dies that the song may live. As
may be seen from a brief, conclusive examination
of his essays, this paradox is of paramount importance in Genet's later writings.

NOTES TO CHAPTER V

[1] Genet, "A Pauvert," in Les Bonnes & L'Atelier d'Alberto Giacometti (Lyon: L'Arbalète, 1958), p. 142.

[2] J.-J. Riniéri, "Genet: Les Bonnes," La Nef, no. 30 (Mai 1947), p. 156.

[3] Lucien Goldmann, "Une pièce réaliste: Le Balcon de Genet," Les Temps Modernes, xv, no. 171 (Juin 1960), 1896.

[4] Pierre de Boisdeffre, Une Histoire vivante de la Littérature d'aujourd'hui (Paris: Le Livre contemporain, 1957), p. 691.

[5] Splendid's is announced as forthcoming in Paul Morihien's checklist of 1945. In his Checklist of 1970, Richard Coe provides this additional information:

On May 7th. 1964 Marc Barbezat wrote to R.W.F. Wilcocks, who was currently writing a thesis on Genet:

"Splendid's est une pièce que Genet m'a vendue en 1948 et dont il m'a cédé l'exclusivité. Malheureusement il n'en a écrit que le premier acte, les deux autres ont été abandonnés. Certains éléments de cette pièce seront repris dans la pièce qu'il écrit actuellement, Le Bagne, dont j'ai les droits et dont j'attends le manuscrit pour le faire paraitre."

On February 14th. 1965 Barbezat wrote to Friedrich Flemming, the German bibliophile:

"J'espère publier très prochainement Le Bagne, que Genet termine et auquel il travaille depuis plusieurs années."

<u>Elle</u>, according to Roger Blin (see footnote 13
to Chapter II) is a play about His Holiness the
Pope of Rome.

[6] <u>A Pauvert</u>(L'Arbalète, 1958), p. 147.

[7] Georges Bataille, for example, has declared that
Genet's adolescent heroes exist at a tragic level
comparable to that attained in ancient Greece.
This and similar observations are recorded by
Philip Thody in his chapter on "<u>Deathwatch</u>,"
in <u>Jean Genet: A Study of his Work</u> (London:
Hamish Hamilton, 1968). Mr Thody himself brings
out the Jansenistic resonances in the play.

[8] <u>Les Bonnes</u> (Lyon: L'Arbalète, 1958), p. 104.

[9] <u>Les Bonnes</u>, which Genet remarks in "Comment jouer
<u>les Bonnes</u>," in no way constitues "un plaidoyer
sur le sort des domestiques," has been subjected
to virtuosic analysis by Sartre in an appendix
of <u>Saint-Genet</u>. Thoroughly homosexual in portent,
Sartre's explication appears to derive from a
remark in <u>Notre-Dame-des-Fleurs</u>:

"S'il me fallait faire représenter une pièce
théâtrale où des femmes auraient un rôle,
j'exigerais que ce rôle fut tenu par des
adolescents, et j'en avertirais le public,
grâce à une pancarte qui resterait clouée
à droite ou à gauche des décors durant toute
la représentation."

"En fait," Sartre adds in a footnote, "<u>Les Bonnes</u>
ont été jouées par des femmes, mais c'est une
concession que Genet a faite à Jouvet." (<u>Saint-
Genet</u>, p. 675). Since Genet actually intended
the roles to be played by boys, Sartre contends,
the play may also be viewed as a homosexual
fantasy; the audience does not know if it is
"really" about two maids and their mistress, or
if the whole thing is not some sort of pederastic
travesty.

Les Bonnes incidentally invites a brief comparison with Strindberg's Miss Julie, a play
which J.-J. Riniéri reviews - unfavourably - in
the same article in La Nef. Both plays present
a triangular situation between a mistress and
two servants. In both plays - since Madameness
cannot exist without Servantdom, and inversely -
the status of any one of the three is subjectively
determined, in varying degree, by the opinion of
the others. In both plays an offstage male -
the Count, Monsieur - paradoxically dominates
in absence. Both plays terminate with a species
of suicide rendered psychologically necessary
by the preceding action. Beyond these facile
similarities, however, must be borne in mind
the vast distinctions of historical background
and perspective.

[10] "The first two (plays) have the economy of means,
the tightness of construction, the close inter-
dependence of characters and concentration within
the rigid discipline of the unities which is
characteristic of all that is best in French
classical and neo-classical drama; and their
model and inspiration is probably Sartre's most
effective play, No Exit. Moreover, they are
still fundamentally addressed to the intellect."
Richard N. Coe, The Vision of Jean Genet (New
York: The Grove Press, 1968), p. 225.

[11] See Eugene R. Alesch, "The phenomenon of aesthetic detachment experienced as an operative force
in twentieth-century art, specifically in the
surrealist theatre of Jean Genet and in the surrealist painting of Salvador Dali," Diss. Ohio
University, 1968, passim.

[12] This interpretation is advanced by Lewis T. Cetta,
"Myth, Magic and Play in Genet's The Blacks,"
Contemporary Literature, vol. 11, no. 4(Aug.
1970), pp. 511-25.

[13] Lettres à Roger Blin (Paris: Gallimard, 1966),
pp. 23-4.

[14] Though its ludic properties have rather been ignored by critics, Saïd's paradoxically glorious descent may be seen as a comical inversion of the triumphal aspirations of the normal occidental hero.

[15] As concrete yet theatrical barriers of death, the screens naturally recall the dissolving mirrors through which Orpheus passes in Cocteau's films and play. If one's mirror-image, laterally inverted and thus illusory, is nonetheless a reflection of "life," to pass through the mirror and vanish utterly beyond is evidently to efface the image, thus to die. Though Genet's screens are paper and not glass, these objects are quite comparable to Cocteau's famous mirrors in Orphée.

[16] Les Bonnes (Lyon: L'Arbalète, 1958), p. 61.

[17] "Comment jouer Le Balcon," unpaginated preface to Le Balcon (Lyon: L'Arbalète, 1962). Subsequent references to the text of Le Balcon as reproduced in this edition will be bracketed into my actual text, e.g. (Balcon, p. 61).

[18] Furbank, "Genet's humour," The Listener, lxxii, no. 1861 (Nov. 26, 1964), p. 856.

[19] The Vision of Jean Genet (New York: The Grove Press, 1968), pp. 262-3.

[20] In his celebrated interview for Playboy, Genet has remarked on the type of public he would ideally have chosen for his first novel, Notre-Dame-des-Fleurs:

"...I'd have liked the publisher to bring the book out with a very innocent-looking cover and in a very small edition, about three or four hundred copies, and to have made sure that it fell into the hands of Catholic bankers and people like that."

Playboy, vol. 11, no. 4 (April 1964), p. 50.
The remark is quoted not for its factual content - Notre-Dame-des-Fleurs was indeed published first in just such an edition - but for what it reveals of the intended readers. The remark, incidentally, was made some twenty years after publication of that novel.

[21] The phrase "beau genêt d'Espagne" requires some explanation. In a footnote to Journal du voleur, Genet provides a brief anecdote:

> Le jour même qu'il me rencontra, Jean Cocteau me nomma 'son genêt d'Espagne.' Il ne savait pas ce que cette contrée avait fait de moi. (JV, p. 47)

Genet's use of the word "genêt" is etymologically confusing. The Cocteau anecdote accompanies a portion of Journal in which Genet relates the circumstances of his birth and his discovery of his mother's name - Gabrielle Genet, without the circumflex. The narrator then proceeds to embellish upon the affinity he perceives between himself and "des fleurs de genêt," the yellow flowers of broom which he associates with the Morvan and, curiously, with the murderer of children Gilles de Rais. One notes that there is nothing particularly Spanish about broom; furthermore, the word "genêt" with circumflex derives from the Latin word ginestra. As used by Cocteau, "genêt" more feasibly connotes "genet," the small, sturdy Spanish horse translatable in English as jennet. The sense of jennet is obviously more apposite to the General's remark in Le Balcon. Yet in both the Barbezat and the Gallimard editions of that play, "genet" is spellt with circumflex. Without circumflex, the word - Genet's own name - derives from the Catalan ginet and the Arabic zinete. In both Le Balcon and the Cocteau anecdote, the author would seem to intend "horse." The relevant portion of the Journal, incidentally, is embedded in an account of the narrator's activities as beggar and male prostitute in Spain.

[22] It is interesting that Carmen's language at
this point recalls the terms in which Genet,
in 1950, addressed Leonor Fini: "Le faste de
cette époque...vous vous retenez aux apparences
...je note les éléments d'un théâtre qui se
poursuit - ou s'y prépare? - jusque dans votre
vie quotidienne...vos forçats ont la tristesse
non plus du mal qu'ils vont accomplir...mais
cette légère et profonde mélancolie des hommes
à qui il reste seulement d'organiser comme une
fête une vie qui se place par delà le désespoir."
(Paris: Loyau, 1950)

[23] Genet, Les Nègres (Lyon: L'Arbalète, 1967),
pp. 110-11.

[24] Lettres à Roger Blin (Paris: Gallimard, 1966),
pp. 11-12.

[25] The use of the minuet from Don Giovanni is
curiously appropriate. In Mozart's opera, the
minuet is heard as Don Giovanni attempts to
seduce the peasant girl Zerlina. To further
this aim, he gives a ball to which he invites
numerous village girls and swains and, unwittingly,
the aristocrats Don Ottavio, Donna Elvira and
Donna Anna. Disguised by masks, these latter
are pursuing Giovanni to avenge various blots
cast upon their honour. The minuet itself masks
both the attempted seduction - a rejection of
society's code - and the aristocrats' pursuit,
the formal beauty of the music providing an
ironic contrast to the dancers' purposes. Similar irony, tension and opposition characterise
Genet's use of that dance. (The fact that Blin
substituted a divertimento does not destroy the
parallels of mask, anti-social defiance and re-
taliation extant between the two dramatic works.)

[26] Genet, Les Paravents (Lyon: L'Arbalète, 1961).

[27] See Lettres à Roger Blin, pp. 53-4.

[28]The Screens, trans. Bernard Frechtman (New York: The Grove Press, 1962), p. 201.

CHAPTER VI: THE AESTHETICS OF JEAN GENET

(a) Introduction

        Apprehensible to the reader as aspects
of technique or content, Genet's aesthetics may
be abstracted from his texts by formalist analysis or thematic commentary. The characteristic
dual structures which I have discussed so far
tend initially to set the reader or spectator at
an aesthetic remove from what is told or enacted
in Genet's poems, novels or plays. Until now I
have ignored the thematic content of those texts
which best present doctrinal aspects of the
question: <u>Journal du voleur</u> of 1949, the Letter
to Leonor Fini of 1950, the essays on Cocteau,
Giacometti and Rembrandt of 1952, 1957 and 1968
respectively. The <u>Playboy</u> article of 1964 provides additional material.

        Analyses of <u>Journal du voleur</u> are fair-
ly numerous and mention of that book is included
here with the perhaps vainglorious intent to
elucidate some of them. The <u>Lettre à Leonor Fini</u>,
on the other hand, rich in neo-surrealist associations, is never treated by critics; comments
on the Cocteau and Rembrandt essays are rare.
Common to Genet's musings on Cocteau, Fini and
Giacometti is the notion of the moral stature
of the artist, as reflected in his struggle with
the perilous and individual domain of form. An
unpleasant personal experience recalled in
<u>L'Atelier d'Alberto Giacometti</u> is reproduced in
the Rembrandt essay, printed literally side by
side with Genet's thoughts on Rembrandt's later
works and, it seems, the human condition generally. Common to all four texts is the implicit
suggestion that the mature artist ultimately
disappears behind his work: Leonor Fini, presumably, behind her archetypal convicts' heads,
Cocteau behind his sculptured, elegant style,
Giacometti behind his skeletal bronze beings and
irreducible busts, Rembrandt behind his undif-
ferentiated last portraits. In their preoccupation with the moral relationship between experience, content and form, in their assumption
that art may embrace and preserve all that is

most repellently human, the essays on Cocteau,
Giacometti and above all Rembrandt invite the
concluding epithet "humanist."

(b) The Aesthete: <u>Journal du voleur</u>

          Attempting to define Genet's position
in western culture, Richard Coe has stated that
Genet is both a traditionalist and a writer of
the <u>avant-garde</u>. Justifying his paradoxical
conclusion, Richard Coe observes:

          It is almost as though his actual
          memories stemmed from a period
          some twenty years before he was
          (in reality) born. When he seeks
          a comparison for Our Lady's hair-
          ·style, he remembers those long-
          forgotten <u>cocottes</u>, Emilienne
          d'Alençon and Eugénie Buffet...[1]

Shortly thereafter, and perhaps with less felic-
ity, Richard Coe declares that Genet would have
"found himself at home" in the circles of Wilde
and Lord Alfred Douglas, for "it was Wilde and
Whistler who preached Genet's own doctrines of
aestheticism." Genet, whom Coe declares to be
"the direct spiritual descendant of Oscar Wilde
and Aubrey Beardsley," is, moreover, an aesthete
in reverse. Coe reasons that, like Wilde, Genet
considers "ethics an insignificant by-product of
aesthetics, nature as a pale imiation (or mirror-
reflection) of art, the choreography of gesture
more important than its purpose or achievement."[2]
But whereas Wilde would say that what is beautiful is good, and what is bad is spurious and ugly,
Genet makes of evil the dynamic principle of
beauty itself. The result is that "art and ethics alike are both confounded irretrievably and
lost in a Satanic maelstrom of gestures."[3] It
is not very flattering to Genet to state that art
is in this manner lost; but that is not the point.
Coe concludes that the "honest <u>bourgeois</u> reader"

(one wonders rather, of these neo-Sartrian stereo-
types, why honesty is invariably the prerogative
of the detested <u>bourgeoisie</u>) who recognises beauty
in one of Genet's novels thus inadvertently sub-
scribes to wickedness.

Genet's "doctrines of aestheticism" are
best found in oft-cited passages from <u>Journal du
voleur</u>. Genet's fifth book in prose, and generally referred to as his autobiography, <u>Journal du
voleur</u> is dedicated to Sartre and Simone de
Beauvoir; it was published by an unknown amateur
in 1948, at a time when Sartre was printing the
articles that foreshadow <u>Saint-Genet</u>. From several pages of <u>Journal</u> it would seem that Genet is
writing as an anti-Sartre paradoxically influenced
by him. This paradox is apparent even in the
passage most often quoted as evidence of Genet's
Wildean tendencies: the discussion on the morali-
ty of crime which the author reports having had
with his policeman friend, Bernard:

> Une fois pourtant, il essaya de se
> justifier d'être flic, il me parla
> de morale. Du seul point de vue de
> l'esthétique considérant un acte, je
> ne pouvais l'entendre. La bonne
> volonté des moralistes se brise
> contre ce qu'ils appellent ma mau-
> vaise foi. S'ils peuvent me prouver
> qu'un acte est détestable par le
> mal qu'il fait, moi seul puis déci-
> der, par le chant qu'il soulève en
> moi, de sa beauté, de son élégance;
> moi seul puis le refuser ou l'accepter.
> On ne me ramènera pas dans la voie
> droite. Tout au plus pourrait-on
> entreprendre ma ré-éducation artis-
> tique - au risque toutefois pour
> l'éducateur, de se laisser con-
> vaincre et gagner à ma cause si
> la beauté est prouvée par, de deux
> personnalités, la souveraine.[4]

Three things, in this passage, suggest the presence of Sartre: the rigorous cartesian logic;

the notions of "bonne volonté" and "mauvaise foi;"
and the desire to prove by argument. In his curious "proof" of beauty, Genet with cunning logic
transforms an objective argument into a subjective one; beauty is subjectively perceived. At
first sight, this contention would seem to support
Coe's conclusion; beauty can - Genet does not say
it must - be generated by evil. The argument,
however, is not about art, but about actual deeds;
art - "le chant qu'il soulève en moi" - presumably
happens afterwards. "Ce n'est qu'après le vol, et
grâce à la littérature, que le voleur chante son
geste." (J.V., p. 232) Genet is applying aesthetic
principles to crime, and this should not be confused with his applying them to art.

Wildean aestheticism, as invoked by Coe,
requires that critics make two intellectual efforts; the first being to separate the work and
the artist, the second, to distinguish between
ethics and the work:

> ...I must admit that, either from
> temperament or from taste or from
> both, I am quite incapable of under-
> standing how any work of art can be
> criticised from a moral standpoint.
> The sphere of art and the sphere of
> ethics are absolutely distinct and
> separate...[5]

This did not, of course, mean that the work itself
could not be moral; Wilde's Ballad of Reading Gaol
is unremittingly so, the De Profundis too. The
defense of the Picture of Dorian Gray - a sort
of English Peau de chagrin in which the gorgeous
hero sells his soul for the outward aspect of
eternal youth - shows that book to have its own
ironic ethical conclusion:

> It is finally to get rid of the con-
> science that had dogged his steps
> from year to year that he destroys
> the picture; and thus in his attempt
> to kill conscience Dorian Gray kills
> himself.[6]

Although Wilde states that the moral content of
Dorian Gray is subordinated to artistic ends, the
exemplary end of Dorian himself causes one to
question Coe's assertion that Wilde's Platonism
would have caused him to equate the good with the
beautiful. Dorian Gray is exquisitely beautiful,
but it is quite apparent that he is not, ultimately, good. Beauty results, rather, from the technical perfections of the work itself, and it is
of this sort of beauty that Genet seems to be
thinking when he writes: "De la beauté de son
expression dépend la beauté d'un acte moral."
(J.V., p. 23) Genet, however, is still thinking
in terms of acts rather than art.

The literary intentions professed in
Journal de voleur are, upon the relationship of
life and art, somewhat contradictory. The book
anticipates Saint-Genet inasmuch as it involves a
reconstruction of Genet's past which will suggest
an interpretation of his literary present. Since
language is incapable of fully recapturing the
past, the resultant literary product must necessarily reflect the author's present circumstance:

> Nous savons que notre langage est
> incapable de rappeler même le reflet
> de ces états défunts, étrangers. Il
> en serait de même pour tout ce journal
> s'il devait être la notation de qui
> je fus. Je préciserai donc qu'il
> doit renseigner sur qui je suis,
> aujourd'hui que j'écris. Il n'est
> pas une recherche du temps passé,
> mais une oeuvre d'art dont la matière-
> prétexte est ma vie d'autrefois. Il
> sera un présent fixé à l'aide du
> passé, non l'inverse.
> (J.V., p. 76)

Had the two books been published simultaneously,
such words, from the Journal, might indicate that
Genet is refuting the method of Saint-Genet. With
scant regard for the distinctions of plot and character and the order in which they were composed,
Sartre reconstitutes Genet's childhood, adolescence

and young manhood from the evidence of the texts;
in Journal, Genet moves in the opposite direction.
What is most apparent in this passage however, is
that Genet intends to write a work of art. This
statement is both complemented and contradicted at
the book's conclusion:

> Ce livre ne veut pas être, poursuivant
> dans le ciel son trajet solitaire, une
> oeuvre d'art, objet détaché d'auteur
> et du monde. Ma vie passée je pouvais
> le dire sur un autre ton, avec d'autres
> mots. Je l'ai héroïsée parce que
> j'avais en moi ce qu'il faut pour le
> faire, le lyrisme.
>
> (J.V., p. 285)

In this second passage, Genet is clearly aware of
the "art for art's sake" theory, which he seems to
be rejecting. The myth of Redemption, which he
propounds in another portion of the book, seems
even less suggestive of aestheticism:

> Créer n'est pas un jeu quelque
> peu frivole. Le créateur s'est engagé
> dans une aventure effrayante qui est
> d'assumer soi-même jusqu'au bout les
> périls risqués par ses créatures. On
> ne peut supposer une création n'ayant
> l'amour à l'origine...le créateur se
> charge du poids de péché de ses per-
> sonnages.
>
> (J.V. p. 221)

Genet at this point seems very far from assuming
the defence of aesthetic detachment; according to
Cocteau, who thinks him a moralist, it was this
sense of total moral responsibility for the vaga-
ries of his characters which caused Genet to decline acquaintance with Gide, on the grounds that
his immorality was suspect. It is hard to extract
from such remarks a keen sense of dichotomy
between life and art; Genet's aestheticism,
then, would seem to lie elsewhere.

In <u>Journal du voleur</u>, as in Genet's
first three novels, the narrating "Jean Genet" recounts his own purported adventures from the past
and recent past. Despite - or perhaps because of -
the author's claim in <u>Journal</u>, that he is inter-
preting his present, a certain distance is denoted
between that present, and the past. This separation
is emphasised by Genet's recurrent tendency to describe his immediate activities of scribe: "Mainten-
ant que j'écris je songe à mes amants," he reflects;
or again, in a footnote,

> Le premier vers que je m'éton-
> nai d'avoir formé c'est celui-ci:
> 'Moissonneur des souffles coupés.' Ce
> que j'écrivai(sic)plus haut me le rappelle.
> (<u>J.V.</u>, p. 51)

Vestigial remains of the "frame" of Genet's first
three novels, these interjections both suspend and
reinforce belief; in writing about writing, Genet
creates a sort of double negative with a positive
effect. He forces the reader to recognise the
artificial nature of the fictional enterprise, but
in so doing allows him to accept it <u>as a fiction</u>.
I have endeavoured to demonstrate that this procedure, akin to aesthetic distancing, characterises
almost all of Genet's works. Even in his essays,
particularly <u>Ce qui est resté d'un Rembrandt...</u>,
Genet is constantly interrupting the progress of
his critical text with introspective meditations
on creativity. Practically all his works tend to
place an emphasis on artifice, containing within
their own structures a means for establishing deliberate illusion. Beyond the "art-historical" affinities his works may display with products of
the <u>fin de siècle</u>, the technique of distancing,
thus erecting an illusory barrier between the
realms of art and reality, permits Genet to be
termed an aesthete of technique.

It is not, however, until 1964, with pub-
lication of the unique <u>Playboy</u> interview, that
Genet ventures comments which directly recall
Wilde's dictum: "There is no such thing as a moral

or immoral book. Books are well-written, or badly
written. That is all."[8] In Journal du voleur,
Genet has observed, of his brutish friend Armand,

> Ses impudiques attitudes je ne puis
> dire qu'elles sont à l'origine de
> ma décision d'écrire des livres
> pornographiques...
>
> (J.V., p. 150)

In the Playboy interview, Genet disavows a porno-
graphic aim, preferring poetry instead:

> I think that if my books arouse
> readers sexually, they're badly writ-
> ten, because the poetic emotion
> should be so strong that no reader
> is moved sexually...[9]

It is in the Rembrandt essay of 1968, possibly one
of the last things Genet wrote before turning utterly to politics, that he comes closest to the
Wildean ideal; works of art, he maintains, should
exalt only the most inapplicable of truths:

> C'est seulement ces sortes
> de vérité, celles qui ne sont pas
> démontrables et même qui sont "faus-
> ses," celles qu'on ne peut conduire
> sans absurdité jusqu'à leur extrémité
> sans aller à la négation d'elles et
> de soi, c'est celles-là qui doivent
> être exaltées par une oeuvre d'art.
> Elles n'auront jamais la chance ni
> la malchance d'être un jour appliquées.
> Qu'elles vivent par le chant qu'elles
> sont devenues et qu'elles suscitent.[10]

In Journal, the equivalent pronouncement was still
primarily concerned with moral acts: "L'acte est
beau s'il provoque, et dans notre gorge fait découvrir, le chant." (J.V., p. 23) In the essay
on Rembrandt it is apparent that Genet's ultimate
concern is with the great poetic undemonstrables
which constitute an autonomous, enduring work of
art.

(c)   The Portraitist: A Letter to Leonor Fini

It is natural that Genet's essays, for
the most part consisting of critical musings about
art, should cast further light on his attitude to
creativity. Written between 1950-1968, almost all
treat of the function of the artist; the duality
which characterises Genet's major works is manifest in several.

Genet's first known essays are those
composed in honour of his personal friends Leonor
Fini and Cocteau. The Lettre à Leonor Fini is a
far from luxurious booklet consisting of nine
pages of unnumbered text and ten black-and-white
reproductions. These latter include the portrait
of Genet himself, painted in 1949; a Tête de bagnard; several sphinxes, painted between 1942-1946;
L'Ange de l'anatomie, of 1949; D'un jour à l'autre,
of 1946; and the Petite fille de Giglio.[11] The
paintings may be loosely grouped into three cate-
gories: portraits, dramatic scenes, and a species
of metaphysical still-life in which snails, skulls,
ossified twigs and disquietingly staring eyes are
represented in minute detail and with the obsessive clarity of some nightmares. In the "scenes,"
two or more persons appear mysteriously fixed in
an atmosphere charged with dramatic import; what
the drama - comedy or crime - it is left to the
viewer to imagine. The most recurrent visage in
these works is that of Leonor herself, frequently
depicted as a sphinx. Drama is not absent from
the portraits, whose subjects gaze vacantly into
infinity with a look at once tragic and translu-
cent. It is indeed the oneiric qualities discernible in these works which most relate them to Surrealism, with its fondnesses for fantasy and dream;
one might also comment that Mme Fini's smooth technique and dream-like spatial planes recall the
limpid surfaces and mythical distances of Dali
and Tanguy, while the metamorphoses further
suggest the influence of Ernst and his curious
"Loplop" birdmen.

Genet's achievement in the Lettre, however, is not to link Leonor Fini with Surrealism,
but rather to canonise the artistic expression of
several of his own favourite themes as he discerns
them in her work. The essay begins by evoking the
"pestilential odour," of plagues and poisons min-
gled, seemingly exhaled by the paintings. One recalls, in this connection, the narrator's fondness
for smells as expressed in Notre-Dame-des-Fleurs:
"J'ai déjà dit comme j'aime les odeurs. Les odeurs
fortes de la terre, des latrines, des hanches
d'arabes et surtout l'odeur de mes pets..." (O.C.
II, p. 97) Smell naturally connotes atmosphere,
and atmospheric associations bind all the themes
discussed: the myth of the Renaissance, with its
dramas of incest, poison and assassination; the
ominous "silence" of the canvases; the part of
fantasy; the taste for opulence and splendour, as
manifest in the sumptuosity of style. These elements are - in Genet's disposition - both related
and subordinate to the themes of criminality and
sanctity, with which the essay culminates:

> Il existe un domaine moral. C'est
> en définitive le seul qu'il importe
> à l'artiste de découvrir par le moyen
> des formes... Pour parler vite,
> c'est vers la sainteté qu'à travers
> votre oeuvre nous désirons vous voir
> vous acheminer.[12]

There is nothing surrealistic in this wish, which
recalls passages from Journal du voleur; indeed,
Mme Fini herself feels that Genet has rather over-
emphasised the moral aspects. It is in examination of more truly Finian themes - of personal
metamorphosis, or the myth of the Renaissance -
that surrealist elements in the two artists' work
may best be compared.

Two motifs distinguish Genet's treatment of the Renaissance as it occurs in his first
two novels: an almost gothic fascination with
poisons, and a more sober architectural predilection for Renaissance castles. Of the two, it is

the former which appears the more "surrealist,"
and also the more Finian. In <u>Notre-Dame-des Fleurs</u>,
one of Culafroy's melodramatic habits is to ad-
minister himself a daily dose of aconite. Poison,
for Genet, is Elixir of Renaissance, a magic potion of quasi-anthropomorphic powers both fatal
and ressuscitative:

> Mais le poison avait la double vertu
> de tuer et de ressusciter d'entre
> les morts ceux qu'il tua, et, preste,
> il agissait. Par la bouche, la
> Renaissance prenait possession de
> l'enfant comme l'homme-Dieu de la
> fillette qui, en tirant la langue,
> avale l'hostie. Les Borgia, les
> Astrologues, les Pornographes, les
> Princes, les Abbesses, les Condottieri,
> le recevaient nu sur leurs genoux
> durs sous la soie, il posait tendre-
> ment sa joue contre une verge érigée,
> de pierre inébranlable, comme doit
> l'être sous le satin nacré de leur
> casaque la poitrine des nègres du
> jazz.
>
> C'était dans une alcôve verte,
> pour des fêtes que termine la mort
> en forme de poignards, de gants par-
> fumés, d'hostie scélérate...
> (<u>O.C. II</u>, p. 74)

Salient in this passage is the element of erotic
profanation, as though the potion were an amorous
anti-Host. At once deadly and resurrective, Culafroy's aconite is an intermediary between two
worlds, between the "real" death it deals and the
world that lurks beyond the real. This, at least,
is how it seems to function for the writer of the
text, and in this sense the poison has eminently
"surreal" powers. For Culafroy himself, it is the
utterance of magic formulas which works the miracle: "Datura fastuosa, Datura stramonium, Bella-
donna..." (<u>O.C. II</u>, p. 74) The surrealist concept
of words as autonomous, enchanting entities is

thus suggested in the passage. Genet alludes
again, albeit briefly, to the Renaissance of
poisonous princesses in Miracle de la Rose:

> Ce siècle est décidément le siècle
> soumis aux poisons, où Hitler est
> une princesse de la Renaissance,
> pour nous une Catherine de Médicis
> muette et profonde, et mon goût
> pour les poisons, l'attrait qu'ils
> exercent sur moi, me fait parfois
> me confondre avec l'une ou avec
> l'autre.
>
> (O.C. II, p. 313)

The comic travesty of Hitler is somewhat reminiscent of the "Hitlerian nurses" painted by Dali in
the late thirties; but the mention of poison is
almost isolated, not really incorporated into the
body of the novel. In Notre-Dame-des-Fleurs, however, Culafroy-Divine's early contact with the
"surreal" may be interpreted as a factor in the
invisible, destructive influence Divine exerts
as an adult.

The terms Genet uses to describe the myth
of the Renaissance as depicted in Mme Fini's oils
strikingly recall those employed in the aconite
episode of Notre-Dame:

> L'époque que vous vivez, c'est
> la Renaissance, je veux dire que
> vous illustrez un thème qui, histor-
> iquement se nomme Renaissance Italienne.
> Le faste de cette époque est celui même
> de votre oeuvre, voluptueuse et sau-
> poudrée d'arsenic. Vos dames allongées
> dans l'alcôve, leurs garçons élégants
> sont emprisonnés, sont atteints d'une
> peste venue de la plus haute antiquité.
>
> (L.L.F.)

One notices again the ubiquitous poison, the al-
coves, the air of elegance, the current of eroticism - ingredients supplemented, on a succeeding

184

page, by those of "silence, crime, inceste, poison,
mort, venin, odeur." (L.L.F.) The paintings to
which Genet most probably refers are La Chambre
noire of 1931, and D'un jour à l'autre of 1946.
In the former, a pale, intense young woman, in-
explicably attired in a damaged Renaissance
breastplate, dominates the foreground; behind her
two young persons are reclining on a bed partly
hidden in an alcove. Clothes litter the floor.
As usual, the drama is felt rather than explained.
D'un jour à l'autre is an implicitly sapphic scene
in which an oddly bedraggled assortment of young
ladies exchange pregnant glances in a marbled
pool. In the background two men are languishing,
visibly the worse for wear, one in fact pecked by
chickens. His sorry state, and tht title, allude
humorously to domesticity. A dilapidated Renaissance is evoked by the shattered arches of the
formal architectural setting. One searches in
vain in these paintings for actual phials of poison or bejewelled daggers; such literality would
be inimical to their mood, which portends the inexplicable and the amusing. Once again, it is the
oneiric dimension of the scenes which best invites
the term "Surrealist."

At this point it is necessary to draw
several firm distinctions between the two artists.
Since Genet's acquaintance with Mme Fini did not
flourish until 1948-9, and since Miracle and Notre-
Dame were written in the early forties, it is improbable that either person influenced the other,
at least where the Renaissance is concerned.
Clearly, Genet is not choosing to evoke the humanis-
tic Renaissance of Marsilio Ficino and Lorenzo de
Medici. His sources, rather, would seem to be the
popular novels to which he refers in Miracle,
particularly the Pardaillan saga of Michel Zévaco,
in which an extravagant Renaissance is peopled by
Catherine de Medici, the Duc de Guise, and a
whole host of Italian astrologers, plotters, poi-
soners, persecuted Huguenots, courtesans and
wicked priests.[13] Leonor Fini, on the other hand,
as an Italian paintress educated in Italy could
scarcely fail to be aware of the various traditions

of the Italian Renaissance. Furthermore, it
would be most unwise to argue that Genet's work
is retrospectively illumined as Surrealist in the
light of the Lettre. What is of interest is the
extent to which he identifies with her; surrealist
resemblances are incidental to that identification,
and must be compared with this in mind.

It is conceivable, however, that Genet
was influenced by knowledge of surrealist work in
the use he makes of metamorphosis in his third and
fourth novels. For Leonor Fini, as for her friend
Ernst, metamorphosis is the logical visual expression of a private myth. Ernst's "Loplop" bird of
the early thirties is a sort of avian alter ego, a
consequence of the artist's "hallucinatory identification" with his feathered friends. Leonor Fini
has always adored cats and wishes to become one;
the result is the sphinx, a legendary beast composed of woman and large cat, and a favourite motif
in her paintings of the forties. Sphinx Amalburga
of 1942, Divinité chtonienne of 1947 and Stryges
Amaouri of 1948 all depict feline women - elegant
beasts, and beautifully groomed - watching over
nude dormant men. Being only demi-bestial, the
sphinx represents an ideal animal combination of
fantasy and fact, an aspect which attracts Mme
Fini more than the creature's fabled oracular
capacity. As for Genet, an instance of feline
metamorphosis occurs in Pompes funèbres, which
he wrote between 1944 and 1947. The description
of this phenomenon is at once so gruesome and so
comic as to suggest that Genet - not renowned as
a cat-lover - is writing as the anti-Fini. Tor-
mented by hunger in occupied Paris, the novel's
adolescent hero Riton decides to kill and eat a
stray grey cat: "L'assassinat," warns the narrator, "fut atroce." Faint with horror and want
of food, fearing the animal to be the devil in
disguise, Riton eventually subdues the beast with
a hammer. A most unappetising meal simultaneously renders Riton ill and effects a partial metamorphosis:

> ...depuis ce jour Riton connaît la
> présence en lui d'un felin qui marque

186

> son corps et plus précisément son
> ventre, comme ces animaux brodés d'or
> sur les robes des dames d'autrefois.
> ...Il avait des gestes si prestes et
> parfois si nonchalants que lui-même
> se croyait quelquefois animé par le
> chat qu'il portait en lui...la
> présence en lui du chat pouvait
> faire Riton se croire transformé, dé-
> formé, exhalant une odeur de felin.
> (O.C. III, p. 103)

It is improbable that Genet could have revolved
in Cocteauesque circles at this time without hear-
ing of Mme Fini's legendary collections of cats,
and Riton's fusion with the beast seems like an
ironic response to the paintress' whimsical mythology. Nonetheless, Genet's cat exacts a posthumous,
fantastical revenge for having been consumed for
so practical a reason. Genet manifests a similar
irony in the Letter of 1950, when led to question
the profundity of Leonor Fini's personal trans-
mogrifications:

> Vous allez au bal masqué, masquée d'un
> museau de chat, mais vêtue comme un
> cardinal romain - vous vous retenez
> aux apparences afin de ne pas laisser
> la croupe du sphinx vous envahir et
> des ailes et des griffes vous pousser.
> Sage prudence; vous me paraissez au
> bord de la métamorphose. Mais si vous
> tolérez le moindre conseil je vous
> donnerez celui de vous retenir moins
> longtemps au monde des humains pour
> regagner les rêves où vous appellent
> vos soeurs les nymphes prisonnières
> du lierre. Ne croyez pas, Leonor,
> que je plaisante: cessez le jeu des
> apparences: apparaissez.
> (L.L.F.)

In intimating a timidity on the part of Mme Fini
with regard to actual metamorphosis, Genet appears
to controvert that lady's usual critics who contend that fantasy and fact are but one in her life.

Genet returns to the question of fantasy slightly
later in the essay. His comments show him to be
quite aware of the distinction between revery and
dream, a distinction significant in Surrealist
theory:

> Mais je parlais de rêve.
> Votre oeuvre semble lui appartenir,
> mais pas tout à fait. Elle relève
> plutôt, me semble-t-il, de la rêverie
> vague et vaguement dirigée, tantôt
> vers le végétal et tantôt vers les
> formes de culture les plus raffinées.
> S'il vous était assez facile de broder
> à partir de ces rêveries, d'inventer
> des formes et d'imaginer des scènes,
> à partir de ces têtes rasées, il me
> semble que votre conscience devra
> être plus grande, votre attention
> plus réfléchie.
> (L.L.F.)

In suggesting that Leonor Fini's "consciousness"
might be enlarged by a less sophisticated play of
illusion, Genet appears to recommend two alternatives: that she abandon herself more fully to
the bestiary of dream - that is, to the autonomous
structures of the sub-conscious; or that she engage in a more lucid examination of herself.
(The two alternatives are not, for the Surrealists,
mutually exclusive, but could be reconciled in the
oneiric state of "hallucination volontaire.")[14]
Although he never specifically quotes Surrealism,
Genet is in effect advocating a more authentically
surrealist approach, at least where dream is concerned.

By a further curious irony, Genet would
seem acutally to have influenced Leonor Fini inasmuch as she started painting convicts' heads after
their collaboration on La Galère in 1947. Her
Têtes de bagnard of 1950 exhibit the dominant
traits of her "imaginary" heads of later years; to
wit: the clear but troubled gaze, the grimly reso-
lute yet pathetic facial expressions which reveal

an intimate dimension in their subjects' struggle
with existence. While not absolutely devoid of
the coquetry which marks most Finian personnages,
such heads have qualities both personal and uni-
versal. They meet with increased approval from
Genet, for he observes: "J'ai la maladresse d'y
voir la recherche d'un dépouillement physique,
mondain, en faveur d'une richesse intérieure."
He does not - unless, again, he is ironic - seem
to envisage an inspiration drawn from his own
work: "Quant à ces forçats, quant à ces galériens
rasés, d'où viennent-ils?" he asks, indicating
subsequently that the artist must have drawn
them from some inner region of the self:

> ...Car je ne puis croire qu'ils ne
> servent qu'à l'ornement de vos jeux.
> Ils ne sont pas prétexte mais fin.
> Trop de pathétique s'exprime par
> les yeux paradoxalement clairs et
> creux où, dans ceux de l'un d'eux,
> vous avez mis le plus angélique
> azur...
>
> (L.L.F.)

Once again, Genet's terms of enthusiasm recall
words from Notre-Dame-des-Fleurs: one thinks particularly of the photographs in the narrator's
cell, "ces belles têtes aux yeux vides" - handsome
heads with vacant, sky-blue eyes and a somnambulistic stare. (O.C.II, p. 10) The gaze is, of
course, a distinctive trait in all Finian portraits, and it is less the treatment than the subject matter which would seem to have been culled
from Genet. While these heads display none of the
fantastical embellishments of such Surrealist portraits as Dali's head of Eluard, they do suggest
a stage in the creation of a myth. It is an interesting footnote to the discussion that Genet's
own portrait has in this connection been though
to be surreal:

> ..en (lui) s'accomplissent les trans-
> mutations du réel en un sur-réel,
> les étapes de la métamorphose,

>l'accession de l'individuel au mythol-
ogie. Mythologique, que cette révéla-
tion de l'autre soi, campé dans
l'inconscient, que cette angélicienne
expression de martyre foudroyé qu'il
y a dans le portrait de Jean Genet... [15]

Naturally this does not mean that Genet's actual
person is "surreal;" it is merely that his mythical likeness being in a sense a convict's head coincides with the myth of the imaginary portraits.
It seems, moreover, logical to conclude this comparison with mention of the portrait, itself a
form of art combining art and life, and a testimony to the association of the paintress and the
poet.

Genet's Lettre à Leonor Fini, therefore,
following upon an acquaintance of several years'
standing, focuses upon the shared themes of criminality, the Renaissance myth, and metamorphosis.
It further touches upon the two artists' preoccupations with death, ceremony and that aspect of ceremony which takes the form of a predilection for
magnificence of style. These latter elements,
however, so predominate in Genet's writing as to
rather overflow the relatively narrow channel of
Mme Fini's "influence." In the domain of themes
shared, it must be admitted that surrealist elements and resemblances, while indubitably present,
are almost accidental; Genet's knowledge of Surrealism, at least until the end of the war, was
probably acquired chiefly through his reading Cocteau. As for Mme Fini's effect upon the poet, it
would seem to have been more social than artistic
- an amusing, if only partial, repatriation of the
outcast via the frivolous, virtually "gratin"
fringes of Surrealist circles. Yet Genet's Letter
does both evince an awareness of the visual aspects of Surrealism and remind the reader of tendencies in the poet's own work which, if not Surrealist in the full historical sense, may certainly be termed neo-surrealist.

(d)   The Humanist: The Essays on Cocteau, Gia-
      cometti, Rembrandt

        Following upon a discussion of structu-
ral and aesthetic characteristics in Genet's literary work, the term "humanist," with its classical and philosophical overtones, may appear oddly,
if not invalidly, applied. It is indeed a rather
peculiar application of the word, justified by the
progression in Genet's thought from the Cocteau
essay, "Grec...!" of May 1952 to the meditation on
Rembrandt which appeared in Tel Quel in 1967.

        Although the Lettre à Leonor Fini attests
principally to Genet's interest in the visual arts
and also to a familiarity with certain aspects of
neo-surrealism, it is connected to the Cocteau
essay by the theme of moral fibre in the artist,
to be acquired through a lifelong struggle with
his or her art:

                Il existe un domaine moral. C'est
                en définitive le seul qu'il importe
                à l'artiste de découvrir par le moyen
                des formes. Mais c'est le domaine
                moral le plus périlleux et le plus
                noble qui nous intéresse - quant à
                sa noblesse, aucune loi pré-existante
                nous renseigne sur elle, il nous faut
                l'inventer. Et c'est toute notre vie
                que nous devons conformer - rendre
                conforme - à cette invention.[16]

In the Fini monograph, this moral domain is still
termed sanctity; in Genet's tribute to Cocteau,
the moral endeavour of the artist is linked, via
the Hellenistic associations conjured forth by the
elder poet's work and person, with the moral marble
of antiquity:

                Grec! La sèche élégance de ce
                mot, sa brièveté, sa cassure même,
                un peu abrupte, sont des qualités
                qui s'appliquent avec promptitude à
                Jean Cocteau. Le mot est déjà un

précieux travail de découpage: ainsi
désigne-t-il le poète dégagé, dépris
d'une matière dont il a fait voler les
copeaux. Le poète - ou son oeuvre mais
donc lui - reste un curieux fragment,
bref, dur, étincelant, cocassement
inachevé - comme le mot grec - et qui
contient les vertus que je veux
dénombrer.[17]

The virtues in question, it transpires, are precisely those half-recognised but also half-ignored by
the words "grace, elegance, charm" habitually applied to Cocteau with a touch of intellectual con-
descension. Insisting upon the profundity of the
elder poet's inner drama, Genet maintains that the
perfection of form and style involves a moral struggle of the highest order: "Je vous engage à tenter
de rechercher, mot à mot, ligne après ligne, le
cheminement sévère - parallèle - de la pureté
d'écriture et de la droiture morale."[18] Continuing
the sculptural metaphor with which the essay opens,
Genet contrasts the mason, who works with stone,
to the poet who, using words, nonetheless creates
marble; Cocteau's verbal matter, he concludes,
constitutes a new moral marble.

In L'Atelier d'Alberto Giacometti, published in 1958, Genet connects the theme of man's
condition with the labours of the artist, the link
between the two being a certain type of nostalgia.
Deploring the vulgar delimitations of the visual
world, Genet hints at the possibility of an inner,
secret realm contained within the self, access to
which might have permitted "une aventure humaine
toute différente." The value of man's inhuman
mortal lot resides, however, precisely in the feel-
ing of nostalgia it induces; the significance of
Giacometti's work, for Genet, derives from its
perception of this contradiction:

C'est l'oeuvre de Giacometti qui me
rend notre univers encore plus in-
supportable, tant il semble que cet
artiste ait su écarter ce qui gênait

> son regard pour découvrir ce qui
> restera de l'homme quand les faux-
> semblants seront enlevés. Mais à
> Giacometti aussi peut-être fallait-
> il cette inhumaine condition qui
> nous est imposée, pour que sa
> nostalgie en devienne si grande
> qu'elle lui donnerait la force de
> réussir dans sa recherche.[19]

The nostalgia mentioned here is itself dualistic,
for it implies an almost Platonic dichotomy between the inhuman world of appearance and the
inner, human realm attained through art. Closely
connected, in this essay, to the theme of the
artist's quest is the theme of solitude, a royal,
irreplaceable solitude located at the core of being
and manifest as a wound into which each human person seeks periodically to withdraw. Giacometti's
sculptures, to which Genet attributes the power of
revealing this royal, secret wound, have the additional merit of restoring to each figure or thing
sculpted its primal sense of solitude. In the
terminology of Genet's essay, Giacometti's art is
profoundly and precisely human.

L'Atelier d'Alberto Giacometti anticipates the major themes of Genet's last articles
and essays. The notion that an artistic object
is destined for posterity is energetically rejected by Genet, who maintains, on the contrary, that
the proper public for the work of art is to be
found among the innumerable legions of the dead;
as a corollary to this proposition, he relates
how Giacometti once conceived the idea of burying
a statue. Applied with grisly humour to the problems of theatrical production, this idea recurs in
1968 in the late essay L'Etrange mot d' ..., a
macabre and "urbane" critique of modern technologi-
cal society in which Genet proposes that theatrical representation be conducted in local urban
cemeteries. With perhaps a lesser degree of humour,
this same concept inspires the Lettres à Roger
Blin of 1966. From these letters it appears that
performance of Les Paravents is intended to create

a poetic conflagration which will blaze beyond the
confines of mortality:

> Afin que cet événement - la ou les
> représentations - sans troubler
> l'ordre du monde, impose là une
> déflagration poétique, agissant
> sur quelques milliers de Parisiens,
> je voudrais qu'elle soit si forte
> et si dense qu'elle illumine, par
> ses prolongements, le monde des
> morts - des milliards de milliards
> - et celui des vivants qui viendront
> (mais c'est moins important.)[20]

To the theme of the dead audience is related the
theme of the dead artist - the creator who has
disappeared behind his creation, or who has died
that it may live. This theme, too, is anticipated
in the Giacometti essay when Genet relates an observation made by Sartre on the sculptor's intention: "Son rêve serait de disparaitre complètement
derrière son oeuvre. Il serait encore plus heureux
si c'était le bronze qui, de lui-même, s'était
manifesté."[21] Similar themes recur in Le Funambule, another essay which Genet published in 1958,
and which he dedicated to his lover Abdallah, a
young tightrope artist. Predominant in this essay,
in fact, are the themes of solitude and death,
conditions necessary to the artist and paradoxically obtained by his solitary, perillous performance high above the heads of his living audience.
"Il s'agit, tu l'as compris, de la solitude mor-
telle, de cette région désespérée et éclatante où
opère l'artiste," writes Genet, advising Abdallah
that death must precede his actual appearance on
the wire; "Celui qui dansera sera mort - décidé à
toutes les beautés, capable de toutes."[22] These
depictions of the artist at his mortal task recall
two brief quotations from Miracle de la Rose:
"L'auteur d'un beau poème est toujours mort," and
"L'oeuvre flambe et son modèle meurt."[23] Beyond
that, the mythical figure of the artist thus
evoked inevitably suggests the myth of the
Phoenix, the fabled bird destined to rise from
the ashes of its own immolation.

More relevantly "humanist," however, is
the theme of human egality which occurs embryonically in L'Atelier d'Alberto Giacometti. Towards
the middle of that essay, the writer recalls an
episode which took place in a train some four
years previously, when his gaze unwittingly met
that of a repulsive little dirty aged man. As a
result of this experience, "Genet" came to the dis-
agreeable realisation that one human life is
pretty much worth another: "...je connus soudain
le douloureux - oui, douloureux sentiment que
n'importe quel homme en 'valait' exactement...
n'importe quel autre."[24] In 1967, Genet published
in Tel Quel an expanded version of this incident,
republished in 1968, remarkable for its typographical disposition and for its title: Ce qui est
resté d'un Rembrandt déchiré en petits carrés bien
réguliers et foutu aux chiottes. While the left-
hand column of the Gallimard edition recounts the
writer's reflections on the experience, the right-
hand column briefly traces the career of Rembrandt,
together with Genet's meditations on the portraits:
"Aussi délicat que soit son regard, la Fiancée
juive a un cul. Ça se sent. Elle peut d'un moment à l'autre relever ses jupes. Elle peut
s'asseoir. Elle a de quoi."[25] Coincidental with
Genet's far from aesthetic discovery of human
equality comes his discovery, no less disconcerting, that the portraits Rembrandt painted in his
later years to not resemble anyone:

> Plus je les regardais, et moins ces
> portraits me renvoyaient à quelqu'un.
> À personne. Il me fallut sans doute
> assez longtemps pour arriver à cette
> idée, désespérante et enivrante: les
> portraits faits par Rembrandt (après la
> cinquantaine) ne renvoient à per-
> sonne d'identifiable.[26]

As a consequence of this reflection, Genet is led
to conclude that it is precisely Rembrandt's
"depersonalisation" of his models which invests
them with the greatest stature. In order to
arrive at this paradoxical investiture, Genet

reasons, Rembrandt had first to accept the human
facts of existence:

> Mais il a fallu que Rembrandt se
> reconnaisse et s'accepte, comme un
> être de chair - que dis-je, de chair?
> - de viande, de bidoche, de sang, de
> larmes, de sueurs, de merde, d'intel-
> ligence et de tendresse, d'autres
> choses encore, à l'infini, mais aucune
> niant les autres ou mieux: chacune
> saluant les autres.[27]

The term "humanism" as applied to Jean Genet would
seem best understood if one bears in mind this implicit and ultimate acceptance of the human person
in its various aspects, repellent and agreeable.

Asked, in his Playboy interview of 1964
whither he intended to direct the current of his
life, Genet blandly replied: "Towards oblivion.
Most of our activities have the vagueness and
vacantness of a tramp's existence. We very rarely make a conscious effort to transcend that
state. I transcend it by writing."[28] In 1970,
at the close of his interview concerning the
Black Panthers, Genet was asked if he intended
writing any more. The response, though ambiguous, seems to imply a negative:

> I don't think Brecht did anything
> for Communism, nor do I think that
> the Revolution was instigated by
> Beaumarchais' The Marriage of Figaro.
> I also think that the closer a work
> comes to perfection, the more self-
> enclosed it is. Worse that that:
> it induces a feeling of nostalgia.[29]

It is an ironic, though not an unfitting conclusion to Genet's literary enterprise that the
circle is complete; from obscurity to oblivion,
the writer is stepping out of sight behind the
works of man.

NOTES TO CHAPTER VI

[1]Richard N. Coe, The Vision of Jean Genet (New York: The Grove Press, 1968), p. 313.

[2]Coe, p. 92.

[3]Coe, p. 93.

[4]Journal du voleur (Paris: Gallimard, 1949), p. 204. Henceforth references to this edition will be inserted into the text under the abbreviation J.V.

[5]Oscar Wilde, "To the Editor of the Saint James Gazette," 25 June 1890. Reproduced in The Artist as Critic: Critical Writings of Oscar Wilde, ed. Richard Ellmann (New York: Random House, 1968), p. 237.

[6]"Letter to the Editor of the Daily Chronicle," June 30, 1890, reproduced in Ellmann, p. 246.

[7]Oeuvres Complètes, IV (Paris: Gallimard, 1968), pp. 268-9.

[8]Preface to The Picture of Dorian Gray in The Portable Oscar Wilde (New York: The Viking Press, 1946, reprinted 1967), p. 138. The remark was quoted at Wilde's trial.

[9]Playboy, XI (April 1964), p. 51.

[10]Ce qui est resté d'un Rembrandt déchiré en petits carrés..., in Oeuvres Complètes, IV, p. 21.

[11]Reproductions of Leonor Fini's paintings mentioned in this chapter are to be found in Jelenski's Leonor Fini (Geneva: Clairefontaine, 1968) and in

Marcel Brion's <u>Leonor Fini et son oeuvre</u>
(Paris: Pauvert, 1955).

[12]<u>Lettre à Leonor Fini</u> (Paris: J. Loyau, 1950),
unpaginated edition. Subsequent references to
this text will be indicated by the abbreviation
<u>L.L.F.</u>

[13]<u>Miracle de la Rose</u>, in <u>O.C. II</u>, pp. 329-30.

[14]See Mary Ann Caws, <u>Surrealism and the Literary
Imagination</u> (The Hague: Mouton & Company, 1966),
pp. 52-3.

[15]Marcel Brion, <u>Leonor Fini et son oeuvre</u> (Paris:
Pauvert, 1955), unpaginated.

[16]Jean Genet, <u>Lettre à Leonor Fini</u> (Paris: Loyau,
1950), unpaginated.

[17]Jean Genet, "Grec!..." <u>Empreintes</u>, Brussels
(May-July 1950), p. 23.

[18]<u>Empreintes</u>, p. 5.

[19]<u>L'Atelier d'Alberto Giacometti</u> in <u>Les Bonnes
& L'Atelier d'Alberto Giacometti</u> (Décines:
L'Arbalète, 1958), p. 10.

[20]Jean Genet, <u>Lettres à Roger Blin</u> (Paris:
Gallimard, 1966), p. 11.

[21]<u>L'Atelier d'Alberto Giacometti</u>, p. 36.

[22]<u>Le Funambule</u> in <u>Les Bonnes & L'Atelier d'Alberto
Giacometti</u>, pp. 180, 184.

[23]<u>Miracle de la Rose</u> in <u>Oeuvres Complètes, II</u>
(Paris: Gallimard, 1951), pp. 359, 397.

[24]L'Atelier d'Alberto Giacometti, p. 23.

[25]Jean Genet, Ce qui est resté d'un Rembrandt déchiré en petits carrés bien réguliers et foutu aux chiottes in Oeuvres Complètes, IV (Paris: Gallimard, 1968), p. 22.

[26]Ce qui est resté d'un Rembrandt..., p. 26.

[27]Ce qui est resté d'un Rembrandt..., p. 28.

[28]Playboy, vol. 11, no. 4 (April 1964), p. 53.

[29]"Jean Genet chez les panthères noires," Express, no. 983 (11-17 mai, 1970), p. 24. Translated by Richard Seaver as "Jean Genet and the Black Panthers," Evergreen Review (November 1970), p. 72.

CONCLUSION: FUNCTIONS OF THE DUAL STRUCTURE

> Et il va de soi que
> toute l'oeuvre de Rembrandt
> n'a de sens - au moins pour
> moi - que si je sais que ce
> que je viens d'écrire était
> faux.
>
> Jean Genet,
> <u>Ce qui est resté d'un Rem-</u>
> <u>brandt déchiré en petits</u>
> <u>carrés bien réguliers et</u>
> <u>foutu aux chiottes</u>.

In concluding a discussion of dual structures as they occur in Genet's works, it seems pertinent to assess the functional significance of
these structures, and the significance of those
themes to which they are so frequently connected.
In Genet's early works - that is to say, the poems
and novels ostensibly composed in diverse peniten-
tiaries - parallels may be drawn between the incarcerated circumstances of the poet and the essen-
tially captive state of his imaginary characters.
The term "dual structures" as it applies to Genet's
writing reflects this parallelism inasmuch as an
inner structure, given as oneiric or illusory, is
contained within an outer framework, presented as
objective fact. In the creative act, an inversion
is effected whereby the poet paradoxically asserts
his liberty as author. The majority of Genet's
later works are comparably structured in a frame,
inversion or interaction of the two structures being not infrequent. The double structure is the
basic formal dominant of almost all his writings.
A genetic approach - the pun is unavoidable - as
applied to Genet's work attempts to explain the
creation of such structures.

In certain books by Genet - most notably
the novel Notre-Dame-des-Fleurs - the inner, imaginative narrative is presented as a deliberate work
of artifice. Attention is thus drawn, naturally,
to the theme of creativity itself. Creativity requires a form of expression, and it is significant
that Genet's first effusions took the form of verse.
In his first poem, Le Condamné à mort, the creative
voice appears to emanate not from the poet but from
Maurice Pilorge, for whom the poem was composed:
song - an elegiac, moribund effusion - emerges as
the elegiac artifice by which the poem lives. In
Marche funèbre, the second poem obsessively concerned with Pilorge, the poet seems to be singing
as himself; embellished by a precious eroticism,
the auto-analysis of his poetical obsessions causes
poetic composition to emerge as the poem's eventual
theme. Similarly, in Notre-Dame-des-Fleurs, an in-
audible refrain permeates the double framework of
the novel. Presented as a balletic, imponderably

lyrical saga - "la Divine-Saga" - the story of
Divine occupies the "inner" portions, the outer
structure being the narrating "Jean Genet's"
account of how he comes to write the book in
prison. Despite a close and necessary interde-
pendence, the two fictions in a sense negate each
other: the oneiric adventures of the inner narrative are generated by the narrator's reveries
in prison, in other words by his internment in
the cell. In driving his creatures to relentless
doom he paradoxically assumes control of his own
literary destiny.

        In Notre-Dame-des-Fleurs, Genet's lite-
rary eclecticism is manifest in the influences of
Cocteau, Proust and Jouhandeau - authors whom
Genet apparently admits to having read. The poet's
Proustian themes - the anachronistic workings of
memory, reflections on artistic sensibility and
creation of the novel as a literary theme - are
most apparent in his first two novels; the influence of Cocteau - indicated, in early works, by
Genet's predilection for such trappings of arti-
face as self-conscious illusionism and the trompe-
l'oeil persists, mitigated it is true, even into
Genet's late plays. As for Jouhandeau, the ironic
mysticism of La Jeunesse de Théophile accords well
with Genet's own fond fusion of things sacred and
profane. Eclecticism itself, one notes, implies
duality in that disparate cultural components are
fused in the given author's individual style. If,
as the Russian Formalist Bhaktine observed, literary works are constantly engaging in an intertex-
tual dialogue with preceding works, eclecticism is
not unrelated to parody in that acquaintance with
a predecessor and a present model is in both instances implied. In Notre-Dame-des-Fleurs parody
- biblical parody - is of a literary species; in
Genet's later works, most notably Le Balcon, it
has a social import. Even in the dramas, however,
parody is dependent for its effect on the cherished
trompe-l'oeil and the interplay of Genet's double
structures of theatrical illusion.

        In Genet's third poem, Le Galère, although

present as a quality of structure, duality is
more perceptible as an attribute of image: the
titular slave galley is both fantastic vessel
and French central prison transformed by that
fantasy. Duality is, moreover, present as a
slightly irritating quality of language, the poem's
major themes - oneiric departure and erotic release - being obscured in a capricious flow of
arch preciosity and argotic hermeticism. Rendered
somewhat inaccessible by the eccentricity of its
composition - two unrelated poems having been
welded together for greater density of sense -
La Galère is nonetheless interesting for its thematic connections with Genet's second novel,
Miracle de la Rose. Both works are dominated by
the mythicised figure of the killer Harcamone;
central passages of the novel concern the narrator's
oneiric departure on a galley from the reformatory
of Mettray. It is in Genet's poems and first two
novels that his affinities with the nineteenth
century appear most clearly. The theme of the
slave-ship itself has Romantic precedents; but as
a metaphorical instrument of quest - at once amorous
and literary in object - Genet's Galère recalls
the poetic departures of l'invitation au voyage,
Brise marine, even of Le Bateau ivre. Genet's
ties with Romanticism, however, are indicated not
merely by resemblances of theme - particularly,
by the intimate relationship of love and death
which so pervades the greater portion of his writing - but also by similarities of structure. The
frame which, modified by cyclic digression, association and interruption, encloses each of Genet's
novels[1] is in certain respects comparable to the
Märchenromane of German Romanticism, in which a
tale is frequently set within an outer frame of
narrative. The effect of this embedding is to
create a double distance between the reader and
the inner frame, emphasising thereby the act of
narration and the imaginative processes entailed.
The Romantic vision, at once ideal and ironic in
perception, is itself dualistic: the frame may be
said to reflect that discrepancy.

        While Genet's novels, poems and plays

practically all observe to some degree the convention of the double structure, the significance
of same is not precisely similar in each. Possibly
the most complex use of the characteristic frame
occurs in Genet's middle novel, Pompes funèbres,
in which a neo-surrealist use of coincidence
unites both the objective and the subjective, the
oneiric inner frame and the objective outer frame.
Just as in Marche funèbre the poet questions the
"hasard" which causes him to write obsessively of
death, the narrator of the third novel is led to
interrogate the biographical coincidence linking
the composition of Notre-Dame-des-Fleurs with that
of Pompes funèbres. This interrogation of chance,
comparable to the artistic declaration of intent
in Breton's Nadja, evinces an awareness of a destiny in which life, coincidence and creativity are
inextricably entangled. As is the case with certain surrealist and neo-surrealist novels, therefore, an implicit unity is posited between man and
his fate.

In four of Genet's five published plays,
a double theatrical illusion, or play within a
play, corresponds to the complex structures of
the novels; in the case of Le Balcon and Les Paravents a prevalent theme of "song" has a double
function in Genet's writings: structurally, it
is a "self-conscious" artifice enabling the work
to declare itself; thematically, it represents
the emotional necessity of uttering imponderable,
undemonstrable inapplicable emotional truths. The
latter necessity is also expressed in Genet's later
theoretical writings, to which I have affixed the
term "humanist." Genet deserves to be called a
humanist in that his writing ventures beyond the
socially acceptable limits of much human experience
and courageously assumes responsibility for whatever it finds there. The moral courage of the
artist, struggling to find the appropriate, enduring form for his work and ultimately disappearing
behind it, is a theme in the earlier essays on
Leonor Fini, Cocteau and Giacometti.

The functions of the double structure

are themselves double and potentially disturbing.
First, one might argue that the double fiction or
double theatrical illusion operates with the seemingly magical logic of the double negative, paradoxically asserting the veracity of the total illusion. Second, one might consider the "metaphysical"
implications of this "vast expansion of the metalepsis," as Gérard Genette has termed the transgressions of Pirandellism:

> D'où l'inquiétude si justement
> désignée par Borges: 'De telles
> inventions suggèrent que si les
> personnages d'une fiction peuvent
> être lecteurs ou spectateurs, nous,
> leurs lecteurs ou spectateurs, pou-
> vons être des personnages fictifs.'
> Le plus troublant de la métalepse
> est bien dans cette hypothèse in-
> acceptable et insistante, que
> l'extradiégétique est peut-être
> déjà diégétique, et que le narrateur
> et ses narrataires, c'est-à-dire
> vous et moi, appartenons peut-être
> encore à quelque récit.[2]

A similar "transgression" would seem to obtain in
Genet's case; the stage effects for the first
tableau of Le Balcon would, precisely, implicate
the spectator in the framework of the play. Here,
however, the reader or spectator does not belong
to another récit, as Genette suggests, but is himself reflected into Genet's universe. Such would
seem to be the ultimate literary irony perpetrated
by the poet-thief whose writing originated and
persisted in the metaphysically troubling, apparently uncontrollable circumstances of a prison
cell.

NOTES TO CONCLUSION

[1] Even in the apparently autobiographical _Journal du voleur_, the author-narrator frequently intrudes upon the recitation of past events, creating by these interruptions a self-conscious narrative present reminiscent of the "absolute" present of _Notre-Dame-des-Fleurs_. Even in _Querelle de Brest_, a novel which appears written in the objective third person, there are intrusions of an authorial "we;" moreover, the subjectively presented, first-person diary of Lt. Seblon corresponds to the narrator's self-conscious ruminations of earlier prose works.

[2] Gérard Genette, _Figures III_ (Paris: Seuil, 1972), p. 245.

BIBLIOGRAPHY

I. EDITIONS OF WORKS BY JEAN GENET

Poetry

Le Condamné à mort. Fresnes, September, 1942.
        Copy with author's MS corrections in
        Bibliothèque Nationale, Rés. p. Ye.
        1561.

Chants secrets. L'Arbalète, n.p. n.d. (=Lyon, 20
        March 1945.) Cover lithograph by Emile
        Picq. B.N. Rés. m. Ye. 529.
        Contains: Le Condamné à mort & Dédicace
                Marche funèbre

La Galère. Paris: J. Loyau, July 1947. Collec-
        tor's edition, with six engravings by
        Leonor Fini. Limited to 80 copies.
        B.N. Enfer, 1612.

Poèmes. Lyon, L'Arbalète, 1966. Reprinted 1966.
        Contains: Le Condamné à mort & Dédicace
                Marche funèbre
                La Galère
                La Parade
                Un Chant d'Amour
                Le Pêcheur du Suquet

Novels and Autobiography

Notre-Dame-des-Fleurs. Monte Carlo, "aux dépens
        d'un Amateur," September 1944. Edition
        limited to 350 copies. B.N. Enfer 1401.

Notre-Dame-des-Fleurs. Paris: Gallimard, 1951.
        In Oeuvres Complètes de Jean Genet, II,
        7-207. Dated "Prison de Fresnes, 1942."
        Reprinted 1967.

Miracle de la Rose. Lyon: L'Arbalète, 30 March
        1946. Edition limited to 475 copies.
        B.N. Rés. 40 Ln. 27. 83466.

<u>Miracle de la Rose</u>. Paris: Gallimard, 1951. In
<u>Oeuvres Complètes de Jean Genet</u>, II, 221-
469. Dated "La Santé. Prison des
Tourelles, 1943."

<u>Pompes funèbres</u>. "Bikini," n.p. n.d.(1947) B.N.
Enfer 1543.

<u>Pompes funèbres</u>. Paris: Gallimard, 1953. In
<u>Oeuvres Complètes de Jean Genet</u>, <u>III</u>,
7-162. Reprinted 1967.

<u>Querelle de Brest</u>. (? Paris, Morihien) December
1947. Edition limited to 1850 copies.

<u>Querelle de Brest</u>. Paris: Gallimard, 1953. In
<u>Oeuvres Complètes de Jean Genet</u>, <u>III</u>,
171-350.

<u>Journal du voleur</u>. "Aux dépens d'un Ami," n.p.
n.d.(1948?) Edition limited to 400 copies.
B.N. Enfer, 1614.

<u>Journal du voleur</u>. Paris: Gallimard, 1949.
Reprinted 1968.

<u>Plays</u>

<u>Haute Surveillance</u>. Paris: Gallimard, 1949.
Reprinted 1965.

<u>Les Bonnes</u>. "Les deux versions précédées d'une
Lettre de l'Auteur." Sceaux: J.-J.
Pauvert, 1954.

<u>Les Bonnes</u>. In <u>Les Bonnes & L'Atelier d'Alberto
Giacometti</u>. Décines: L'Arbalète, 20
May 1958. Also contains: <u>L'Enfant
Criminel</u>; <u>Le Funambule</u>; <u>Lettre à Pauvert</u>.

<u>Le Balcon</u>. Lyon: L'Arbalète, March 10, 1962.
Also contains <u>Comment jouer "Le Balcon."</u>

<u>Les Nègres</u>. Décines: L'Arbalète, 1960. Edition

with 33 photographs by Ernest Scheidegger.
Preceded by Pour jouer "Les Nègres."

Les Paravents. Décines: L'Arbalète, 1961.

The Screens. English translation by Bernard
Frechtman. New York: The Grove Press,
1962.

Articles, Essays and Criticism

'Adame Miroir. Paris: Paul Morihien, 1949,
pp. 37-58. Also Contains L'Enfant
criminel.

L'Atelier d'Alberto Giacometti. With 33 photographs
by Ernest Scheidegger. Décines: L'Arbalète,
1963. Reprinted 1967.

L'Atelier d'Alberto Giacometti. In Les Bonnes &
etc. Décines: L'Arbalète, 1958.

Ce qui est resté d'un Rembrandt déchiré en petits
carrés bien réguliers et foutu aux chiottes.
In Oeuvres Complètes de Jean Genet, IV.
Paris: Gallimard, 1968, pp. 19-31.

Comment jouer "Le Balcon." As in Le Balcon. Lyon:
L'Arbalète, March 10, 1962.

Comment jouer "Les Bonnes." In Les Bonnes & L'Atelier d'Alberto Giacometti. Décines:
L'Arbaléte, 1958.

L'Etrange Mot d' ... In Oeuvres Complètes de Jean
Genet, IV. Paris: Gallimard, 1968,
pp. 7-18.

L'Enfant criminel. In Les Bonnes & L'Atelier
d'Alberto Giacometti. Décines: L'Arbalète, 1958.

Le Funambule. In Les Bonnes & L'Atelier d'Alberto
Giacometti. Décines: L'Arbalète, 1958.

"Grec!...." (Article on Cocteau.) Empreintes (Brussels), May 1950, pp. 23 ff.

J'ai été victime d'une tentative d'assassinat. Arts(Paris), 1 May, 1957.

The Members of the Assembly. Translated by Richard Seaver. Esquire, Nov. 1968, pp. 86-9.

Lettre à J.-J. Pauvert sur Les Bonnes. In Les Bonnes & L'Atelier d'Alberto Giacometti. Décines: L'Arbalète, 1958.

Lettre à Leonor Fini. Paris: J. Loyau, 1950. B.N. 80. V. pièce 31512.

Lettres à Roger Blin. Paris: Gallimard, 1966.

Lettres à Roger Blin. In Oeuvres Complètes de Jean Genet, IV. Paris: Gallimard, 1968, pp. 215-264.

A salute to 100,000 stars. Translated by Richard Seaver. Evergreen Review, vol. XII, No. 61, Dec. 1968, 50-53.

Pour jouer Les Nègres. In Les Nègres. Décines: L'Arbalète, 1960.

Le Secret de Rembrandt. Express, No. 377, 4 Sept. 1958, pp. 14-15.

Something which seems to resemble decay ... English translation of preceding item by Bernard Frechtman. In Art and Literature: An International Review (Lausanne), No. 1, March 1964, pp. 77-86.

Interviews

Playboy, Vol. 11, No. 4, April 1964, pp. 50 ff.

"Jean Genet chez les panthères noires," Express, No. 983, 11-17 Mai 1970, p. 24.

II. THEORETICAL WORKS CONSULTED

Barthes, Roland and Philippe Hamon, W. Kayser and
        W.C. Booth. Poétique du récit. Paris:
        Seuil, coll. Points, 1977.

Culler, Jonathan. Structuralist Poetics. Ithaca:
        Cornell University Press, 1975.

De George, Richard and Fernande, eds. The Struc-
        turalists, From Marx to Lévi-Strauss.
        New York: Doubleday, 1972.

Genette, Gérard. Figures III. Paris: Seuil, 1972.

Ricardou, Jean. Problèmes du nouveau roman.
        Paris: Seuil, coll. Tel Quel, 1967.

Scholes, Robert. Structuralism in Literature.
        New Haven: Yale University Press, 1974.

Todorov, Tzvetan. Poétique de la prose. Paris:
        Seuil, 1971.

_____. Poétique. Paris: Seuil, coll. Points,
        1972.

_____. Théorie de la littérature. Ed. and Transl.
        texts by Russian Formalists. Paris: Seuil,
        coll. Tel Quel, 1965.

Zumthor, Paul. Essai de poétique mediévale. Paris:
        Seuil, 1972.

III. CRITICAL AND OTHER WORKS

Abel, Lionel. "Metatheater: Le Balcon," Partisan
        Review, XXVII, no. 2, 324-330.

_____. Review of Our Lady of the Flowers, New
        York Review of Books, I, no. 4, Oct. 17,
        1963, 7-8.

Alesch, Eugene R. "The phenomenon of aesthetic detachment experienced as an operative force in twentieth-century art, specifically in the surrealist theatre of Jean Genet and in the surrealist painting of Salvador Dali," Doctoral dissertation, Ohio University, 1968.

Attinelli, Lucio. "Genet et l'Italie," Cahiers des Saisons, No. 21, Spring 1960, pp. 50-51.

Barthes, Roland. "Jean Genet: Le Balcon (mise-en-scène de Peter Brook)," Théâtre Populaire, 38, 1960, pp. 96-8.

Bataille, Georges. L'Erotisme. Paris: Editions de Minuit, 1957.

_____. La Littérature et le mal. Paris: Gallimard, 1957, pp. 185-226.

Baudelaire, Charles. Les Fleurs du mal. Paris: Garnier Frères, 1961.

Beauvoir, Simone de. La Force de l'Age. Paris: Gallimard, 1960.

_____. La Force des Choses. Paris: Gallimard, 1963.

Bersani, Leo. "Literature as the Hitlerism of the spirit," The New York Times Book Review, June 15, 1959, p. 5, 16.

Boisdeffre, Pierre de. Une Histoire vivante de la littérature d'aujourd'hui. Paris: Le Livre contemporain, 1957, pp. 277-280; 661-662.

Bonnefoy, Claude. Genet. Paris: Classiques du XXe. Siècle, 1965.

Botsford, Keith. "But he writes like an angel," New York Times Magazine, Feb. 27, 1972, p. 16 ff.

_____. "What's new in the novel," Yale French Studies, 1951, no. 8, pp. 82-92.

Breton, André. Nadja. Paris: Gallimard, 1928.

_____. Manifestes du Surréalisme. Paris: Pauvert, 1962.

Brion, Marcel. Leonor Fini et son oeuvre. Paris: Pauvert, 1955.

Brophy, Brigid. Review of Our Lady of the Flowers, The London Magazine, IV, no. 3, June 1964, 89-94.

Brown, Frederick. An Impersonation of Angels. New York: The Viking Press, 1969.

Caws, Mary Ann. Surrealism and the Literary Imagination. The Hague: Mouton & Company, 1966.

Cetta, Lewis T. "Myth, Magic and Play in Genet's The Blacks," Contemporary Literature, vol. 11, no. 4, Autumn 1970, 511-25.

Clark, Eleanor. "The World of Jean Genet," Partisan Review, XVI, no. 4, April 1949, 442-448.

Cocteau, Jean. La Difficulté d'être. Paris: Morihien, 1947.

_____. Les Enfants terribles. Paris: Gallimard, Livre de Poche, 1966.

_____. La Machine infernale. Paris: Gallimard, Livre de Poche, 1966.

_____. Opéra. Paris: Dutilleul, s.d. (1959).

_____. Poèmes 1916-1955. Paris: Gallimard, 1956.

_____. Thomas l'Imposteur. Paris: Gallimard, 1923.

Coe, Richard N. _The Vision of Jean Genet_. New York: The Grove Press, 1968.

_____. "Jean Genet: a checklist of his works in French, English and German," _Australian Journal of French Studies_, VI, no. 1, 1969, 113-30.

_____. _The Theater of Jean Genet: A Casebook_. New York: The Grove Press, 1970.

Deharme, Lise. _Les Années perdues_. Paris: Plon, 1961.

Dorchin, Auguste. Ed. _Les Cent Meilleurs Poèmes lyriques (de la langue française)_. Imprimé en Angleterre: House of Grant, 24e. édition, 1957.

Dort, Bernard. "Le jeu de Jean Genet: _Les Nègres_," _Les Temps Modernes_, XV, 1959/60, 1875-1884.

Driver, T. _Jean Genet_. Columbia Essays on Modern Writers, 1966.

Elevitch, Bernard. "Sartre and Genet," _Massachusetts Review_, V, 1963-4, 78-85.

Federman, Raymond. "Jean Genet ou le théâtre de la haine," _Esprit_, no. 391, April 1970, pp. 687-713.

Fernandez, Dominique. "Claudel et Genet," _Nouvelle Revue Française_, VIII, 1960, 119-123.

Fowlie, Wallace. _Age of Surrealism_. Indiana University Press, 1960.

Furbank, M. "Genet's Humour," _The Listener_, LXXII, no. 1861, Nov. 26, 1964, 856.

Furst, Lillian R. _Romanticism in Perspective_. London: Macmillan, 1969.

Gauthier, Xavière. _Surréalisme et sexualité_.
        Paris: Gallimard, Coll. Idées, 1971.

Gerber, Barbara L. "Jean Genet: the Writer as
        Alchemist; Metamorphoses in Fiction and
        Reality," Doctoral Dissertation, Universi-
        ty of Wisconsin, 1968.

Gracq, Julien. _Un Balcon en forêt_. Paris: Jose
        Corti, 1958.

Graham-White, Anthony. "Jean Genet and the psychol-
        ogy of colonialism," _Comparative Drama_,
        IV, no. 3, Fall 1970, 218-16.

Graven, Jean. _L'Argot et le tatouage des criminels_.
        Neuchâtel: Editions de la Baconnière,
        1962.

Hanrez, Marc. "Un rituel érotico-guerrier:
        Pompes funèbres de Jean Genet," _Kentucky
        Romance Quarterly_, IV, no. 3, Fall 1970,
        208-16.

Hugo, Victor. _Les Contemplations_. Paris:
        Gallimard, Livre de Poche classique,
        1969.

_____. _La Légende des Siècles, La Fin de Satan,
        Dieu_. Ed. Jacques Truchet. Editions de
        la Pléiade. Paris: Gallimard, 1967.

Jacobsen, Josephine, and William R. Mueller.
        Ionesco and Genet: Playwrights of Silence.
        New York: Hill and Wang, 1968.

Jean, Marcel. _Histoire de la peinture surréaliste_.
        Paris: Editions du Seuil, 1959.

Jelenski, Constantin. _Leonor Fini_. Geneva:
        Editions Clairefontaine, 1968. Re-
        printed Olympia Press, 1972.

Jouhandeau, Marcel. _Algèbre des valeurs morales_.
        Paris: Gallimard, 1935.

_____. La Jeunesse de Théophile. Paris: Galli-
         mard, 1921.

_____. Prudence Hautechaume. Paris: Gallimard,
         1913.

_____. Traité de l'abjection. Paris: Gallimard,
         1937.

Knapp, Bettina. "An interview with Roger Blin,"
         Tulane Drama Review, VII, No. 3, 1963,
         111-24.

_____. Jean Genet. New York: Trewyne, 1968.

Koch, Stephen. "The romantic of the wretched life,"
         Nation, 214, June 12, 1967, 763 ff.

Lamartine, Alphonse de. Méditations poétiques.
         Paris: Larousse, 1942.

Leduc, Violette. La Folie en tête. Paris: Galli-
         mard, 1970.

McMahon, Joseph. The Imagination of Jean Genet.
         Yale University Press, 1963.

Mack, Owen. "The Aesthetic Basis of the Plays of
         Jean Genet," Doctoral Dissertation,
         University of Michigan, 1969.

Magnan, J.-M. Pour un blason de Jean Genet.
         Coll. Poètes d'aujourd'hui. Paris:
         Pierre Seghers, 1971.

Mallarmé, Stéphane. The Penguin Poets. Ed. Anthony
         Hartley. Suffolk: The Chaucer Press,
         1965.

Marcel, Gabriel. "Non, malgré les Sartre et les
         Genet, tout est loin d'être perdu,"
         Nouvelles Littéraires, 26 mai 1960, p. 10.

_____. "Les Nègres: une scandaleuse exploita-
         tion des thèmes à la mode," Nouvelles
         Littéraires, 17 décembre 1959, p. 10.

Mauriac, François. "Le Cas Jean Genet," _Figaro Littéraire_, 26 mars 1949.

Moraly, Jean-Bernard. "Le Théâtre dans le théâtre dans le théâtre de Jean Genet," Thèse de Maitrise, Université de Paris, 1970.

Morand, Claude. "Enfin _Les Paravents_ de Jean Genet," _Arts et Loisirs_, 28, 6-12 avril 1966, p. 17.

Nadeau, Maurice. _Histoire du Surréalisme_. Paris: Editions du seuil, 1964.

Nelson, Benjamin. "Sartre and _Notre-Dame-des-Fleurs_," _The Psychoanalytical Review_, Fall 1963, vol. 1, No. 3. (special issue.)

Obliques, 2. Ed. Roger Borderie and Henri Ronse. Paris: 1972. Special issue devoted to Genet.

Pierret, Marc. "A propos des _Nègres_," _Lettres Nouvelles_, vol. VII, No. 32, Dec. 2, 1959, p. 35.

Poirot-Delpech, B. _Au soir le soir_. Paris: Mercure de France, 1970.

Praz, Mario. _The Romantic Agony_. Cleveland and New York: Meridian, 1933. Reprinted July 1968.

Proust, Marcel. _A la recherche du temps perdu_. Ed. Pierre Clarac et André Ferré. Editions de la Pléiade, 3 vols. Paris: Gallimard, 1954.

Rheims, Maurice. _Kunst um 1900_. Vienna: Anton Schroll, 1965.

Riniéri, J.-J. "Journal du voleur," _Les Temps Modernes_, No. 43, May 1949, 943-5.

_____. "Genet: _Les Bonnes_," _La Nef_, No. 30, May 1947.

Rousseaux, André. "Décomposition littéraire,"
    Figaro Littéraire, 15 sept. 1952, p. 2.

Rubin, William S. Dada and Surrealist Art. London:
    Thames and Hudson, 1969.

Saillet, Maurice. Billets doux de Justin Saget.
    Paris: Mercure de France, 1952.

Saksena, Nita. "A bunch of fairies," Thought,
    (Delhi) XVI, 33, Aug. 15, 1964, 16-18.

Sartre, J.-P. Saint-Genet, comédien et martyre.
    Vol. I of Oeuvres Complètes de Jean Genet.
    Paris: Gallimard, 1952. Reprinted 1970.

Schardt, Hermann. Paris 1900: Masterworks of
    French Poster Art. New York: G.P. Put-
    nam's Sons, 1970.

Thody, Philip. Jean Genet: a study of his novels
    and plays. London: Hamish Hamilton, 1968.

_____. "Four cases of literary censorship."
    Inaugural lecture, Leeds University, 27
    November 1967. Leeds University Press,
    1968.

Tulane Drama Review, 7, 1962. Special issue on Genet.

Ughetti, Dante. "Motivi orfici nel Miracle de la Rose,
    Biblioteca del Archivum Romanicum, 89-91,
    I, 1967, pp. 40-59.

Valéry, Paul. Poésies. Paris: Gallimard, 1966.

Verlaine. Choix de Poésies, Verlaine choisi par
    lui-même. Club des Librairies de France.
    Paris: Fasquelle, 1961.

Wilde, Oscar. The Artist as Critic: Critical
    Writings of Oscar Wilde. Ed. Richard
    Ellman. New York: Random House, 1968.

————. The Portable Oscar Wilde. New York:
      The Viking Press, 1946. Reprinted 1967.

Yale French Studies, 29, spring-summer 1962.
      Special issue on the New Dramatists:
      Genet, Beckett, Ionesco, Montherlant.

Zeltner, Gerda. La Grande Aventure du roman au XXe
      siècle. Paris: Editions Gonthier, 1967.